Holiday!

Credits

Creative Director	Richard Tracy
Copy Director	Marie DeBenedicitis
Copywriter	Linda Skender
Senior Decorator	Amy Rohr
Cake Decorators	Mary Gavenda
	Corky Kagay
	Susan Matusiak
Recipe & Project Consultants	Culinary Arts & Services
Photographer	Kathy Sanders
Photo Assistant	Christy Gozdik
Prop Stylist	Wendy Marx
Production Coordinator	Mary Stahulak
Production	RNB Graphics

Contents

If you have decorated cakes before, you've experienced the joy of doing and delighting. If decorating is something you've always wanted to try but never have, you're in for a real treat. Learning a new talent is always rewarding and the pleasure that this one brings is heartwarming.

We'll tell you what you need to decorate a cake that looks like a vision. All of our ideas will work excellently with your favorite recipes or cake mixes. Our icing recipes are kitchen-tested to insure successful decorating results.

There's alway time to make holiday cookies. No matter how hustling the Christmas bustle gets, we're never too busy to bake batches of those once-a-year yummies, too good to resist. And in the process, make memories that we relish with delight throughout our lives.

Discover how rewarding it is to turn traditional gingerbread dough into unforgettable edible eye-catchers guaranteed to bring joy and create the fondest holiday remembrances forever!

'Tis the season to make it merry with candy centerpieces that steal the show where you live or charming fudge houses to wrap up and give.

You'll find the luscious molded mousse and gelatin desserts divine to serve anytime. Plus mini breads and coffee cakes to please the most persnickety brunch bunch or late-night livelies.

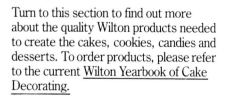

Turn to this section to find out more about the quality Wilton products needed to create the cakes, cookies, candies and desserts. To order products, please refer to the current <u>Wilton Yearbook of Cake Decorating.</u>

Ready-to-trace shapes that will assist you in duplicating many of the projects shown. Easy-to-transfer pattern instructions are included.

Cake Decorating

All Is Merry 'n Bright

This sparkling centerpiece will brighten their spirits and yours. The decorating is so easy, you can even do this glowing ring on the spur of the moment. Try our rich lemon cake recipe or use your favorite pound or yellow cake mix. Serves 14 guests.

You'll need
- 10 in. Ring Mold/Pan
- Decorating Tips 3, 12, 349
- Leaf Green Icing Color
- Disposable Decorating Bag
- Maraschino cherries, drained and patted dry,
- 3 in. diameter pillar candle

Rich Lemon Cake Recipe
1½ cups granulated sugar
2 cups cake flour
2 teaspoons baking powder
1 package (3 ounces) lemon gelatin
¾ cup milk
⅔ cup light cooking oil
2 Tablespoons lemon extract
4 large eggs (separated)

In one mixing bowl, sift 1¼ c. of the sugar, flour, baking powder and gelatin together. In another bowl, combine milk, oil and lemon extract.

Beat the liquids into the dry ingredients until batter is smooth. Beat egg yolks into the batter, one at a time. Whip egg whites until stiff (not dry) with ¼ cup of the sugar. Fold the egg whites, lightly but thoroughly, into the batter.

Grease ring pan with vegetable shortening and dust with flour. Spoon batter into pan and bake at 325°F, 40 to 50 minutes until cake springs back lightly to the touch. Turn out immediately onto a wire rack.

Ice and decorate
Thin buttercream icing to a pourable consistency. Cover cake top with icing. For controlling "drips" so they look picture-perfect, fill a disposable decorating bag with icing and snip off a very small opening. Squeeze icing around top and allow it to run down side at even intervals. Let icing set. Pipe a scalloped vine with tip 3 and green icing. Add tip 349 green leaves. Edge base with tip 12 bulb border. Place cherries around cake top. Position candle in center.

Victorian Tree

Lovely cookie fans romanticize our frilly fir tree cake.
Elegant extras…cut out larger fan cookies for
favors or placecards. Serves 12 guests.

You'll need
- Treeliteful Pan, Cookie Sheets
- Decorating Tips 1, 2, 4, 101, 124
- Leaf Green, Pink Icing Colors
- Buttercream Icing Recipe (p. 16) for cake
- Snow-white Buttercream (p. 13) or Royal Icing Recipes (this page) to decorate cookies
- Roll-Out Cookie Dough Recipe (p. 23)
- Silver dragees

Step I–make & decorate cookies
Using Fan Patterns, cut 9 small and desired number of large cookies. Make slits in dough with the opening of tip 124. Bake and cool. Decorations can be piped with snow-white buttercream or royal (easier to store since it dries hard). Outline curves with tip 1 (smaller cookies) or 2 (larger) strings. Add dots with same tips. Print names with tip 1. Pipe ribbon bows with tip 101. Add dragees (a tweezer would help you place them).

Step II–decorate cake
Ice top and sides smooth with buttercream icing. Edge top with tip 4 bead border. Pipe tip 124 ruffles in rows on trunk and around sides. Trim edge of ruffles with tip 4 beads. Add dragees to ruffles on trunk. Pipe tip 1 dots randomly on cake top and ruffle at base.

Royal Icing
This smooth, hard-drying icing makes decorations that last. Ideal for making flowers, piping figures, overpiping and decorating cookies. Flowers and decorations made from royal icing will last for months, if stored properly, without softening. Royal icing decorations should be air dried. Allow several hours drying time for large decorations. Make sure bowl and utensils are grease free, since any trace of grease will cause royal icing to break down.

Royal icing dries quickly, so keep icing bowl covered with a damp cloth at all times. Store in air tight container. Rebeat at low speed before using.

Note: Royal icing is edible, however, since it dries candy-hard, it is not recommended for icing your cakes. Use only for special effects you want to last.

For piping delicate stringwork or to create a fluffier consistency, add 1 teaspoon of piping gel or light corn syrup to 1 cup icing.

Royal Meringue Recipe
3 level Tbsps. Wilton Meringue
Powder Mix
4 cups sifted confectioners sugar
(approx. 1 lb)
6 Tbsps. water

Beat all ingredients at low speed for 7 to 10 minutes (10 to 12 minutes at high speed for portable mixer) until icing forms peaks. Makes 3 cups

Note: When using large counter top mixer or for stiffer icing, use 1 Tbsp. less water.

Royal Egg White Recipe
3 egg whites (room temperatures)
4 cups confectioners sugar
(approx. 1 lb.)
½ tsp. cream of tartar

Beat all ingredients at high speed for 7 to 10 minutes. Use immediately. Rebeating will not restore texture.

Makes 2½ cups

Christmas Belle

This nostalgic charmer will capture hearts and be the center of attention. Our pretty Wonder Mold Doll cake is clothed in a glamorous "fur-trimmed" costume made of rolled fondant icing. We've included all the patterns you need to make her exquiste hooded cloak and ruffled skirt. Serves 12.

You'll need
- Wonder Mold Kit
- Decorating Tips 1, 233
- Red-Red Icing Color
- 8 in. Cake Circle
- Rolled Fondant Recipe (this page), Buttercream Icing (p. 16), Royal Icing Recipe (p. 6)

Step I—prepare fondant

Rolled Fondant Recipe
1 Tbsp. unflavored gelatin
¼ cup cold water
½ cup Wilton Glucose
1 Tbsp. Wilton Glycerin
2 Tbsp. solid vegetable shortening
2 lbs. confectioners sugar
Red-Red Icing Color.

Combine gelatin and cold water; let stand until thick. Place gelatin mixture in top of double boiler and heat until dissolved. Add glucose and glycerin; mix well. Stir in shortening and just before completely melted, remove from heat. Cool mixture until lukewarm.

Place 1 lb. of the confectioners sugar in bowl and make a well. Pour lukewarm gelatin mixture into the well and stir with a wooden spoon, mixing in sugar and adding additional sugar, a little at a time, until stickiness disappears. Knead in remaining sugar, icing color (tint ¾ of recipe) and flavoring. Knead until the fondant is smooth, pliable and does not stick to your hands. If fondant is too soft, add more sugar; if too stiff, add water (a drop at a time).

Use fondant immediately or store in airtight container in refrigerator. When ready to use, bring to room temperature and knead again until soft. Fondant will be a similar consistency to pie dough.

Step II—ice cake base
Bake cake* in Wonder Mold. Place baked cake on cake circle. Push doll pick into cake. Build up waist with icing for a smooth look and lightly ice cake. So fondant will adhere, keep icing moist by lightly misting.

Step III—dress doll cake
To Roll Out Fondant: Spray work surface and rolling pin with vegetable oil pan spray and dust with a mixture of confectioners sugar and cornstarch.

Roll out fondant into a circle twice the diameter of the pattern. As you roll, lift and move the fondant to prevent it from sticking to the surface. Cut out the bodice pattern pieces (note: to prevent fondant from drying out, cut each piece as it is needed.)

Pick up piece with a spatula. Press pieces onto doll pick, smoothing away "seam" lines. Cut out the underskirt and center it on cake. Cut 2 strips of fondant 1 x 8 in. long for ruffles. Press bottom ruffle on first, "pinch-pleating" it as you go along. Repeat procedure for top ruffle. Each of the pieces you add to the cloak should have a graceful draped effect.

Place skirt of cloak over cake, smoothing back seam and waistline.

Position doll's arm then add each sleeve, the capelet and hood. For muff, cut a 2 in. log-shaped piece of fondant and push in doll's hands. Using royal icing, cover edge of ruffles on underskirt with tip 1 beads. Pipe tip 233 pull-out fur around hood, neckline, capelet, sleeves, skirt, cover her muff.

*We suggest pound with icing or fruitcake with marzipan. Cover finished cake with plastic. Store pound cake up to 3 days; fruitcake up to 1 month.

Candles and Bows

Spruce up your holiday table with this stunning centerpiece tree cake. Fluffy white boughs are dotted with pretty pink icing bows and glowing "candles." This quick-to-decorate standout serves 24 guests.

You'll need
- Holiday Tree Kit
- Decorating Tips 3, 6, 102
- Pink, Yellow, Wilton Red mixed with Burgundy Icing Colors
- Buttercream Icing Recipe (p. 16)
- Uncooked pieces of spaghetti for candles

(Hint: For icing tree, thin icing with a little corn syrup.)

Follow step-by-step baking and assembly instructions included in Holiday Tree Kit.

To Make "Candles:" Break pieces of uncooked spaghetti into 2½ in. lengths (approximately 25). With tip 6 on your decorating bag, gently push the open end down over spaghetti covering 1¼ in. Slowly pull bag up and away. Touch tip 3 to top end and pull out the flame. Push into styrofoam to dry.

With your spatula, generously cover tree with icing. Using a fork, pull icing out in rows working from the bottom up.

Pipe tip 102 swag garlands. Push in "candles." Add tip 102 ribbon bows.

Old St. Nick

Looking absolutely divine in his elegant red robe and cap, trimmed with "ermin." Basic decorating techniques are all you need to know to create this cake of distinction. Serves 16 guests.

You'll need
- Santa Stand-Up Pan
- Decorating Tips 2, 4, 16, 233
- Red-Red, Pink Icing Colors
- Buttercream Icing Recipe (p. 16)

Follow step-by-step baking and assembly instructions included with Santa Stand-Up Pan.

Outline facial features, cap, mittens and robe with tip 4. Cover his face, cap, mittens and robe with tip 16 stars. Pipe tip 16 reverse shell beard. Make eyebrows and mustache with tip 16 shells. Cover cuff and pompon on cap and edge robe with tip 233 pull-out fur. Trim fur with tip 2 swirled beads.

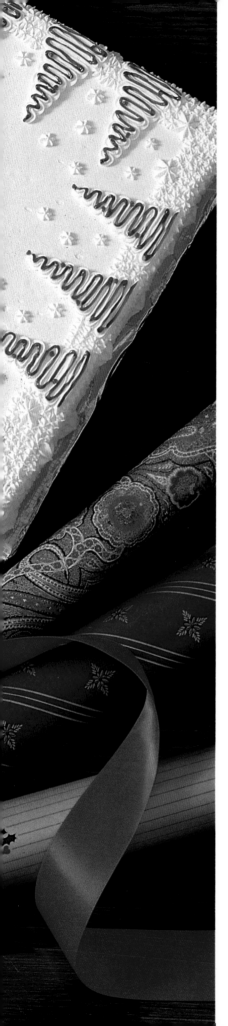

Fantasy Forest

Snow-white icing covers this crowd pleaser like a layer of fresh fallen snow. And what do you know? You can see the forest through the trees. It's such a breeze to do...make two and give one to a friend! Serves 20 guests.

You'll need
- 11 x 15 in. Sheet Pan
- Decorating Tips 1, 16 and 21
- Leaf Green, Christmas Red Icing Colors
- Piping Gel
- Buttercream Icing Recipe (p. 16), 2 needed

Ice cake smooth. With toothpick, mark "Merry Christmas" and Tree patterns (p. 66). Write message with tip 1 red tinted piping gel. Cover the trees with tip 16 zigzags. Around trees, pipe tip 16 stars. Randomly pipe larger stars over small stars with a tip 21. Sprinkle background with tip 16 star "snowflakes." With tinted piping gel and tip 1, trim the trees with green zigzags and red dot ornaments.

Holly Bear

Count on this bear bearing gifts to bring joy to one and all. He'll really tickle them pink with his happy face and bow-tied package. Serves 12 guests.

You'll need
- Huggable Bear Pan
- Decorating Tips 4, 6, 17, 67, 104
- Pink, Christmas Red, Leaf Green Icing Colors

Ice area where gift box will go. With toothpick, mark Gift Pattern (p. 67). Outline facial features, inside of ears, snout, paws and folds of box with tip 4 strings. Pipe in the whites of the eyes and the nose with tip 6 and smooth with your finger (dip in cornstarch to prevent icing from sticking). Add tip 6 dot pupils and flatten with your finger. Cover ears, head, face, paws and body with tip 17 stars. Trim gift with tip 104 ribbon bands. Pipe tip 4 dots randomly on gift. Add tip 104 ribbon bow. At bear's neck and around base, pipe tip 67 leaves. Trim leaves with tip 4 dot berries. Add tip 4 outline lashes to his eyes.

Snow-White Buttercream Recipe
2/3 cup water
4 Tbsps. Wilton Meringue Powder Mix
12 cups sifted confectioners sugar
(approximately 3 lbs.)
1¼ cups solid shortening
¾ tsp. salt
½ tsp. Almond Extract
½ tsp. Clear Vanilla Extract
¼ tsp. Butter Extract

Combine water and meringue powder; whip at high speed until peaks form. Add 4 cups sugar, one cup at a time, beating after each addition at low speed. Alternately add shortening and remainder of sugar. Add salt and flavorings; beat at low speed until smooth.

Makes 7 cups.

Note: Recipe may be doubled or cut in half. If cut in half, yield is 2⅔ cups.

Candy Cane Lane

Jolly figure piped Santas frolic in the icing "snow." One builds a snowman while the others slide down candy cane poles. The figure piped delights can be piped right on the candy canes. Serves 16 guests.

You'll need
- 9 in. Round Pans
- Decorating Tips 1, 5, 9, 10, 12, 13, 16
- Christmas Red, Leaf Green Icing Colors
- Decorating Comb
- Buttercream (p. 13 or 16), Royal (p. 6) Icing Recipes
- Candy canes, red and green sprinkles

Step I—figure pipe standing Santa and snowman with royal icing

For Santa: On waxed paper, pipe tip 5 shoes and tip 9 legs. While legs are setting up, pipe tip 12 body. Push tip 9 into body and squeeze out arms. Add tip 5 hands. Let icing set, then add tip 12 head. When set enough to pick up, position body atop legs. Attach with royal icing. Pipe tip 9 hat and add tip 5 dot pompon. Trim suit with tip 13 zigzag "fur" and face with tip 13 reverse shell beard. Add tip 1 facial features.
For Snowman: Pipe tip 12 bottom snowball, let set. Add tip 12 center ball and tip 9 ball head. Pipe hat and scarf with tip 9. Trim hat with tip 5 dot pompon and tip 13 reverse shell fur. Add tip 1 facial features and buttons.

Step II—decorate cake

Ice two-layer cake smooth with buttercream. With decorating comb, make wavy effect on sides. Edge top and base with tip 10 ball border. With toothpick, mark sides into 8ths. Position candy canes at marks. Edge base with tip 16 zigzag border. Place standing Santa and snowman on cake top. Pipe tip 10 "snow" balls around them and add candy sprinkles.

Step III—figure pipe candy cane Santas with royal icing

For sitting Santa: Hold decorating bag parallel with candy cane. Pipe tip 12 body and head. Push tip 9 into body and pull out legs and arms. Add tip 5 dot hands and shoes. For sliding Santas: With decorating bag at a 45° angle to candy cane, pipe tip 12 bodies and heads. Finish with the same tips that you used for sitting Santa. Trim the same as standing version.

White Christmas Tiers

A stunning spectacular for weddings and winter balls. Silver-centered poinsettias cascade gracefully; delicate stringwork encircles elegantly. It truly has Christmas presence. Serves 87 guests.

You'll need
- 4-Pc. Oval Pan Set
- Decorating Tips 3, 67, 70, 199, 352, 363
- Flower Nail No. 7
- Cake Boards, Dowel Rods, Tuk-N-Ruffle, Fanci-Foil Wrap
- Flower Formers, Florist Wire
- Buttercream Icing (this page) 3 recipes need
  Royal Icing (p. 6) 1 recipe
- Silver dragees

Step I—make royal icing poinsettias and holly leaves

Make 15 poinsettias with tip 352. For each, attach a small square of waxed paper to No. 7 flower nail with a dot of icing. Starting in center of nail, pipe four even petals. Add four more in between, then a row of six in center, shorter and pulled up higher. Add silver dragees in center.

Make 40 holly leaves–25 with tip 70, 5 with tip 67. Thin icing and hold bag at a 45° angle to surface, back of bag facing you. Squeeze and hold tip in place to let icing fan out into base. Relax pressure as you pull tip towards you and draw leaf to a point. While icing is wet, pull out tiny points around edge with a dampened art brush. Let dry on flower formers for a curved look.

To make cake top bouquet, you'll need to make 4 more poinsettias and 5 of each size leaf on wires. For flowers: On waxed paper square, pipe a dot base with tip 4. Make ⅛ in. hook on one end

of 4 in. florist wire and insert hook into base. With slightly moistened art brush, smooth and taper icing on the wire. Push other end of wire into a piece of styrofoam to dry. Remove waxed paper and attach flower to base with dot of icing. For leaves: Lay 4 in. florist wire on waxed paper. Using tips 67, 70, pipe each leaf directly over wire end. Let dry. To form bouquet: Twist wire stems together. Set flowers, leaves and bouquet aside.

Step II—baking, icing and stacking tiers

Use all but the largest oval in your pan set. Fill and ice 2-layer cakes smooth with buttercream icing on cake boards cut to fit. Place bottom tier on Tuk 'n Ruffle-trimmed foil-covered cake board. Dowel rod bottom and middle tier for support. Position middle tier on bottom tier off center. Repeat procedure for top tier. To keep stacked tiers stable, sharpen one end of a dowel rod and push through all tiers and cardboard circles to base of bottom tier.

Step III—decorate

With toothpick, mark garlands on sides– 16 garlands, 2⅜ in. wide, on bottom tier, 12 garlands, 2½ in. wide, on middle and 12 garlands, 1⅞ in. wide, on top. Pipe tip 363 upright shells at marks. Connect shells with tip 3 triple drop strings. Trim with silver dragrees. Edge bases with tip 199 shell borders. Accent cake tops with tip 363 reverse shell borders. Position flowers.

Buttercream Icing Recipe
½ cup solid vegetable shortening
½ cup butter or margarine*
1 tsp. Clear Vanilla Extract
4 cups sifted confectioners sugar
(approx. 1 lb.)
2 Tbsps. milk**

Cream butter and shortening with electric mixer. Add vanilla. Gradually add sugar, one cup at a time, beating well on medium speed. Scrape sides and bottom of bowl often. When all sugar has been mixed in, icing will appear dry. Add milk and beat at medium speed until light and fluffy. Keep icing covered with a damp cloth until ready to use. For best results, keep icing bowl in refrigerator when not in use. Refrigerated in an airtight container, this icing can be stored 2 weeks. Rewhip before using. Makes 3 cups

*Substitute all-vegetable shortening and ½ teaspoon Wilton Butter Extract for pure white icing and stiffer consistency.

**Add 3-4 Tbsps. light corn syrup per recipe to thin for icing cake.

Cookies & Gingerbread

12 Days of Christmas
Centerpiece Tree

*Proud partridge perches gracefully over fluttering fowl,
maids-a-milking, gold rings, drummers' drums, pipers'
notes, lords a leaping and more. Patterns (page 67-71)
included make it easy to cut out cookie boughs and
trims. Birds, rings and notes are figure piped
with royal icing.*

You'll need
- 14 in. Cake Circles (2 needed)
- Fanci-Foil Wrap
- Decorating Tips 1, 2, 3, 6, 8, 12, 16, 67
- Icing Colors: Brown, Wilton Red, Kelly Green, Royal Blue, Golden Yellow, Creamy Peach
- Gingerbread Family Cutter Set
- Cake Dividing Set
- Grandma's Gingerbread (2 recipes needed, p. 32)
- Royal Icing Recipe (p. 6)
- 1 styrofoam cone – 12 in. high, 5 in. diameter base
- Round toothpicks or bamboo skewers
- Paring knife
- Non-toxic marker
- Waxed paper
- 8 miniature marshmallows

Step I – make gingerbread, cut and bake.

Make patterns out of waxed paper (see p. 80).

Roll out gingerbread dough to ¼ in. thickness (use 1 recipe for tree, the other for trims). Lay patterns on dough and cut around them with a paring knife. Hint: Roll dough out on cookie sheet to eliminate transferring from counter. For tree: Cut 12-in. circle for base; one each 11, 10, 9, 8, 7, 6, 5, 4, 3 and 2 in. rings. For trims: 2 partridges, 9 drums (drummers), 19 small gingerbread ladies (8 maids and 11 ladies), 12 small gingerbread boys (lords)

Bake separately in a preheated 350° oven for 10 to 14 minutes or until done (smaller pieces will take less time).

Step II – assemble tree
Make royal icing recipe. Frost entire cone with brown icing (¼ cup). Cover two cake circles with foil wrap (see p. 80). Attach 12 in. cookie base with royal icing to foil-covered base.

Place 12 in. base and rings on cake dividing set and with a non-toxic marker, mark off intervals that correspond to the cookie's size – 12 in. has 12 intervals, 11

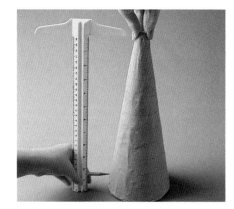

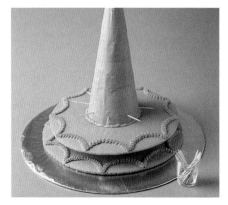

in. has 11 and so on. Hint: For marking the larger cookies, the Cake Dividing Set marking wheel is very helpful.

With green royal icing, connect marks with tip 16 zigzag garlands. Pipe deep enough for decorations to fit. Let dry. Also edge 12 in. cookie with zigzags. Let dry.

So cookie rings sit level on cone, with toothpick mark intervals using Cone Pattern (p. 68). Center cone on 12 in. base cookie and attach with icing. Push 6 wooden sticks into cone where 11 in. ring will go. Be sure picks are pushed in level not at an angle.

Place the 11 in. ring onto cone. If necessary, adjust picks so the ring is level. If the center hole needs to be enlarged, carefully cut the hole by pressing gently with knife blade. Don't use a sawing motion. To secure ring, pipe a line of brown royal icing between cookie and cone with tip 3.

Repeat procedure until all rings are positioned on cone. Adjust the number and length of picks used to support each ring.

Step III – decorate cookie trims and figure pipe icing decorations
Use our Royal Icing Recipe, p. 6

Let outlines dry, before flowing into areas.

Cookie Decorating
Partridge: Tip 3 red outlines. Tip 3 yellow fill in beak. Tip 13 light brown stars. Tip 2 blue dot eye. Tip 13 green pull-out star wreath with tip 2 red dots.

Maids-A-Milking: Tip 2 blue outlines (let dry). Tip 2 blue and white flow in. Tip 1 white dot eyes and red outline mouth. Tip 13 yellow pull-out stripe hair. Marshmallow "bucket" (attach with dots of icing) and tip 2 red handle.

Drums: Tip 2 red outlines. Tip 2 white and blue flow in. Tip 2 yellow zigzags and red strings.

Ladies: Tip 2 peach outlines and flow in dress. Add tip 1 facial features, blue zigzag trim and belt. Add tip 13 yellow curls.

Lords: Tip 2 red outlines and flow in suits. Tip 1 facial features. Tip 2 gold zigzag banner. Tip 13 gold shell epaulets. Tip 13 light brown hair.

Figure Piping

Pressure is the key in successful figure piped decorations. Use heavier pressure in areas you want to build up dimension. When tips are listed, the larger tips are used to form body and head; small tips are for facial features. See picture for colors.

Make	Tips
2 turtle doves	6, 2, 1
3 French hens	6, 2, 1
4 calling birds	6, 2
5 gold rings	12
6 geese with eggs	6, 3, 2
7 swans	6, 2
10 musical notes	8
4 pears	6, 2, 67

Step IV—trim the tree

To attach partridge to tree top, ice back of one partridge with royal icing and position two wooden picks so that they extend from bottom of cookie. Press on the other partridge. Let dry. Push into styrofoam cone so that the partridge is facing out.

Pipe tip 16 zigzag water where swans will go. Use tip 6 to dot back of cookie and icing trims to secure to tree. Be sure to space them evenly around the boughs within the garlands.

Cookie Luminarias

Shimmer, glimmer, glow. These dazzlers will brighten any room. Make several! They're perfect for gifts. And just think what bake-sale best sellers they will be.

You'll need
- Large Cookie Sheets
- Decorating Tips 3, 16, 102, 352
- Wilton Red, Kelly Green Icing Colors
- Star Cutter Set, Gingerbread Family Cutters
- 12 in. Cake Circle, Fanci-Foil Wrap
- Roll-Out Cookie Dough, 2 recipes needed (this page)
- Chocolate Cookie Dough, (p. 41)
- Royal Icing Recipe (p. 6)
- Clear hard candy (lollipops, sour balls or open-centered candies)
- 1¼ in. tall candle in clear holder

Step I—make & bake
Cover cookie sheet with aluminum foil. Spray with vegetable oil pan spray. Roll cookie dough on cookie sheets to ⅛ in. thickness. Cut out pieces using Luminaria Side Pattern. You'll need 6 side panels for each. With cookie cutters, cut out desired shapes in side panels. Carefully remove dough inside of cut-out shape.

For stained glass: Place pieces of candy in heavy plastic sandwich bags (you'll need ¼ cup of 3 different colors). Crush coarsely with a hammer. Note: Larger chunks are used to trim side seams of the gingerbread people design. Fill openings of cookie pieces with ½ to 1 teaspoon of candy (add more for larger openings). Mound candy in center of opening (don't spread it out). Carefully place cookies in oven and bake at 325°F for 9 to 11 minutes. Allow pieces to cool for 5 minutes before removing from cookie sheets. Using a wide, thin spatula, remove cookies.

Step II—assemble
Cover 12 in. cake circle with Fanci-Foil Wrap (see p. 80). Center Floor Base Pattern on circle and trace shape with a

non-toxic marker. Using royal icing (as a "mortar") and tip 16, cover marks and attach panels together. If necessary, support panels with a jar or can until icing has hardened.

Step III—decorate
Top: Edge stars with tip 16 scrolls. Overpipe with tip 3 red outlines. Edge tops and sides seams with tip 16 reverse shells; base with shells. Trim with tip 3 dots. Add tip 352 leaves and tip 3 dot berries.

Center: Use Chocolate Dough Recipe (p. 41). Edge stars with tip 16 scrolls. Cover top and side seams with tip 16 reverse shells. Edge base with tip 16 shells. Trim with tip 3 dots.

Bottom: Outline gingerbread cut-outs with tip 3. Ice side seams smooth and cover with candy chunks. Edge top and base with tip 16 shells. Pipe tip 102 ribbon bows.

Roll-Out Cookie Dough Recipe
1 cup butter
1 cup sugar
1 large egg
2 tsp. baking powder
1 tsp. vanilla
2¾ cups flour

In a large bowl, cream butter and sugar with an electric mixer. Beat in eggs and vanilla. Add baking powder and flour, one cup at a time, mixing after each addition. The dough will be very stiff; blend last flour in by hand. Do not chill dough. **Note:** Dough can be tinted with Icing Color. Add small amounts until desired color is reached.

Preheat oven to 400°F. Divide dough into 2 balls. Roll out on lightly oiled cookie sheets to ⅛ in. thickness. Use a lightly floured rolling pin. Lay prepared pattern pieces lightly on rolled out dough and cut around edges with sharp knife or use cookie cutters (dip in flour). Leave at least 1 in. space between pieces. Pick up the scraps around cut pieces and wrap in plastic wrap to reroll later.

On top rack of oven, bake large pieces about 12 minutes, checking frequently so edges do not brown. Small shapes bake 6 to 8 minutes. Remove immediately to wire racks to cool.

To store: Wrap any unused dough tightly in plastic wrap and refrigerate. Bring to room temperature and knead briefly to use again. Makes about 2 dozen large cookies.

Season's Greeting Cards

Here's a unique way to get your message of good cheer across loud and clear. This cookie greeting card will tell them you're glad they're there and that you really care.

You'll need
• Cookie Sheets
• Decorating Tips 1, 3, 5, 13, 16
• Snowman, Rudy Reindeer or any other Christmas cutter shape
• Oval Cookie Cutter Set
• Decorator's Brush, Decorating Comb
• Candy Melts – White & Christmas Mix
• Christmas Tree & Bell Candy Molds
• Roll-Out Cookie Dough (1 recipe yields 2 cards), this page
• Royal (p. 6) & Buttercream (p. 13 or 16) Icing Recipes
• Corn syrup

Step I – make & bake cookie dough
Grease cookie sheets and roll out dough on sheet to ⅛ in. thickness. Cut 6 card patterns. For card front, center largest oval or rectangle opening pattern, and cut out shape. Cut out snowman and reindeer. Bake 8-10 minutes. Remove from oven and cool on rack.

Step II – assemble cards
Generously ice one side of card backs with buttercream icing. Note: For longer lasting decorations, ice with royal icing. Make wavy effect in icing with decorator comb. Place fronts and backs together.

Step III – decorate
With a Decorator's Brush, lightly cover card fronts with light corn syrup. Let dry before decorating. This will prevent the grease in cookie from discoloring the icing. Mold tree and bells out of melted coating. Let set. Decorate snowman and reindeer with royal icing using tip 3 for outlining and fill-in; tip 16 to cover with stars.

For bas-relief cookie cards: Place snowman and reindeer inside of ovals. With thinned royal icing, outline front, around outer edge and oval opening with tip 3. Let outline set, then flow in icing with tip 3 or cut bag. When set, trim outer edges with tip 16 shells. Edge ovals with tip 3 beads or tip 13 shells. Trim shells with tip 3 dots. Add messages with tip 1.

For candy-trimmed cards: Attach tree and bells with melted candy. With royal icing, write tip 1 message and bows. Trim frame with beads – tip 3 around center, tip 5 on outer edge.

Chocolate Cookie Tree

This dramatic centerpiece will turn everyone into stargazers.
With our rich chocolate cookie dough and elegant ganache
recipes, not only does it look spectacular—
it taste delicious.

You'll need
- Christmas Cookie Tree Kit
- Cookie Sheets
- Candy Melts™* (1 bag White, 2 bags Light Cocoa for Ganache)
- Decorating Tip 3
- 10 in. Cake Circles
- Chocolate Cookie Recipe (make 3 recipes p. 41)
- Ganache Glaze Recipe (make 2 recipes)

Step I—make, cut and bake cookies
Divide dough recipe into two balls. Roll one ball at a time on floured surface. Dough should be ¼ in. thick. For larger stars, roll out on cookie sheet, then cut. Hint: Place dampened towel under cookie sheet to prevent sheet from slipping as you roll out dough.

Cut out two of each size star plus one extra of the smallest size to stand on top of tree. Hint: Make extras in case of breakage.

Bake cookies on top rack of oven for 6 to 7 minutes (larger cookies may take longer) or until cookies are set. Bake cookies of similar sizes on same cookie sheet, so they will finish baking in the same length of time. Remove from cookie sheets to wire racks with a large spatula. Cool about 30 minutes. Cover a flat surface with paper toweling and place baked pieces on it to dry overnight.

Make a base for your tree following directions on page 80.

Step II- Glaze stars & stack

Ganache Glaze Recipe
1 cup whipping cream
14 oz. package Light Cocoa
Candy Melts*

Pour whipping cream into 2-quart glass measuring pitcher. Microwave at 70% power for 2½ to 3 minutes or until hot. Remove and stir in Wilton Candy Melts until melted. If Ganache is not thick enough to pour, let set a few minutes.

To glaze: Place cookie stars on a cake rack over drip pan. Pour the glaze over each cookie starting in center and working toward edges with spatula; be sure to cover sides. Let dry completely, approximately 1 hour. Excess glaze can be reheated and poured again.

To stack: First position largest iced star cookies atop one another, alternating points, using melted Candy Melts as the "glue". Continue to build upwards, adding medium and small iced cookies in the same manner. The smallest iced cookie is reserved and used for trimming the top of the tree.

Step III—decorating
Melt white Candy Melts according to directions on package. Drizzle candy on tree with tip 3 and outline reserved star. Let set. Attach star to top with dots of melted coating.

*brand confectionery coating

Fireside Chat

The stockings are hung on the fireplace with care in hopes of bringing lots of adoring stares. Candy logs are set aglow with icing flames. On the mantel, a unique set of candleholders. The "stone" front is a vision right out of a childhood dream.

You'll need
- Cookie Sheets
- Oval Cookie Cutter Set
- Decorating Tips 3, 16, 352
- Brown, Wilton Red, Kelly Green, Golden Yellow Icing Colors
- 12 In. Cake Circles, Fanci-Foil Wrap
- Grandma's Gingerbread Recipe (p. 32)
- Royal Icing Recipe (p. 6)
- Birthday candles (3 needed)
- Candy trims: open-center hard candies, chewy chocolate rolls, peppermints, candy-coated chocolates, gum drops, jelly patties, mint leaves, hard and rock candies, jelly beans, square chocolate covered dessert mints, small cinnamon candy

Step I—make, cut & bake gingerbread
Make pattern pieces according to directions on p. 80. Prepare cookie sheets and roll out dough according to recipe directions. With patterns (p. 70), cut 5 pattern pieces for fireplace. Using largest oval cutter, cut out rug. Gently press the smaller cutters into dough to make impressions to follow when decorating. Bake and cool.

Step II—assemble & decorate
While gingerbread bakes, make stockings (2 needed) and flames. Trace patterns (p. 69) onto waxed paper. Use royal icing and outline patterns with tip 3. Fill in stockings with tip 3 and pat down with finger dipped in cornstarch. When outlines around flames have dried, fill in–place thinned red royal icing in a

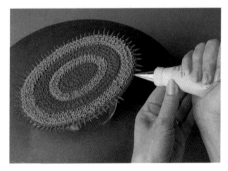

disposable bag and snip off end. Let flames and stockings set until hard.

Place two cake circles together and cover with Fanci-Foil Wrap (see p. 80).

To assemble fireplace: Draw guidelines on cake circle where sides and back will be. Pipe tip 3 lines on marks and position back of fireplace; attach sides and front piece by piping icing on the edges. Support pieces with a jar or can until icing hardens completely. Pipe around top and gently press mantel in place. The back of this piece should be flush with the back of the fireplace to create a slight overhang in the front and on sides. Let dry overnight.

Step III—trim the fireplace
With spatula, spread a layer (½ in. thick) of white royal icing over top of mantel. Position dessert mint squares. To attach hard candies to fireplace: With brown-tinted royal icing, pipe a generous dot of icing on each candy and cover all sides of fireplace (back is optional). When dry, attach stockings.

For candleholders, attach open-center candies together with icing. Cut candles to fit the varying heights and place through centers. Stack chewy chocolate rolls "logs" and add flame. Trim mantel and stocking with tip 352 leaves and tip 3 dot berries. Attach candles with icing.

Attach rug to circle with dots of royal icing. Outline with tip 3 and cover with tip 16 stars. Edge with tip 3 pull-out dot fringe. Let dry.

Festive Cookie Containers

Here are two attractive ways to serve your Christmas goodies.

A Gingerbread Bowl
Everything's edible, right down to the plate.

You'll need
- Wonder Mold & 12 in. Round Pans
- Decorating Tips 1, 2, 3, 13, 18
- Red-Red, Kelly Green, Brown, Golden Yellow Icing Colors
- Cookie Cutters in the Gingerbread House Kit or Gingerbread Family Cutters
- Spritz Cookie Press
- Grandma's Gingerbread Dough (1 recipe), p 32
- Royal Icing Recipe (p. 6)

Step I—make, cut and bake gingerbread
For plate: Roll dough, then cut a 12 in. diameter circle (use a 12 in. cake circle as your guide). Bake 15 minutes and cool.

For bowl: Cover outside of Wonder Mold with aluminum foil and grease lightly. Preheat oven to 375°. On waxed paper, roll out a circle of gingerbread, 12 in. diameter. To place dough on pan, center Wonder Mold with narrow end down on gingerbread. Center pan, on circle, lift dough and pan together and turn pan over. Remove waxed paper. Smooth out any folds or wrinkles, if necessary, cut a slit in dough to remove excess. Bake for 15 to 18 minutes or until edges are lightly browned. Remove from oven and immediately cut dough off 1 in. above base. Allow dough to cool on pan, then remove.

For cookie kids & Santa: Cut out boys and girls (12 needed around bowl) and one Santa. Bake and cool.

Step II—assemble bowl & decorate
Ice bottom of bowl with royal icing and place in center of plate. Edge bowl and

plate with tip 18 zigzag garlands. Trim with tip 2 dot berries.

To decorate kids: Outline outfits with tip 3. Flow in with thinned icing (allow each color to set, before piping another). Add tip 3 hair and tip 1 faces. For Santa: Outline and flow in outfit and cap with tip 3. Pipe tip 3 outline belt. Edge cap and suit with tip 13 zigzags. Add mustache, beard and pompon with tip 13. When cookies dry, stand them around bowl. Fill your bowl to the rim with cookies or candy.

Holly Cookie Tray
A merry berry way to serve up sweets!

You'll need
- 9 in. Hexagon Pan
- Decorating Tips 3, 5, 12
- Kelly Green, Red-Red Icing Colors
- Cake Circles, Fanci-Foil Wrap
- Holly, Rudy Reindeer and Cottage Cookie Cutters
- Roll-Out Cookie Dough, 2 recipes (p. 23)
- Royal Icing (p. 6)

Step I—make, cut and bake
Lightly grease pan. Preheat oven to 375°. Reserve ¼ of dough and tint the rest green. Press dough into bottom of pan, bringing it up the sides approximately ¾ in. Bake for 15 minutes. Cut out 6 holly leaf trios (out of green dough); one or more Rudy Reindeer, cottage and snowman. Bake 7-10 minutes. Cool base and cookies on a wire rack.

Step II—assembling & decorating
Attach holly to sides of base with royal icing. Edge seam inside tray with tip 5 green icing beads. Pipe tip 12 red bulb border around base. Add tip 5 red ball berries to holly. Outline cookies with tip 3 royal icing string. Place on tray.

Cookie Box Santa

Shape this jolly, happy soul out of gingerbread dough and receive compliments galore. Bake or buy a variety of pretty spritz cookies and fill him to the brim. Make two boxes— one to keep, the other to give.

You'll need
- Jolly Santa Pan & Oval Pan Set
- Decorating Tips 4, 8
- Spritz Cookie Press (includes a delicious Spritz Cookie Recipe)
- Grandma's Gingerbread Dough (this page)
- Royal Icing Recipe (p. 6)
- Jelly patties, candy-coated chocolates, cherry ball, red decorator sugar

Step I—make and bake gingerbread
Grease pans. Preheat oven to 375°F. For lid and bottom: Roll dough out to ¼ in. thickness, using pan as a guide to size.

Carefully press dough into Santa pan, starting at the top and working down to try to eliminate air bubbles. Bake for 17 to 20 minutes or until edges begin to pull away from the pan. Turn out onto a rack to cool. Repeat procedure to make another Santa face for bottom of box.

For sides of box: Roll gingerbread out into 2 in. wide strips. Gently press strips around inside of greased oval pan. Smooth seams when adding a new strip. Bake sides 10 to 13 minutes.

Step II—assemble box and decorate
For bottom half of box, place face side down and attach sides with royal icing. Ice sides smooth and pat with red sugar.

For lid: Ice Santa's cap, then pat with red sugar. With tip 4, pipe eyes, brows and nose, outline cuff of cap, pompon, lashes and beard, print "cookies." Edge base of box with 8 bead border.

Hint: To fill with a festive favorite, use our Spritz Cookie Press. It includes a delicious recipe and let you squeeze out a variety of holiday shapes.

Grandma's Gingerbread Recipe
5 cups all-purpose flour
1 teaspoon baking soda
1 teaspoon salt
2 teaspoons ginger
2 teaspoons cinnamon
1 teaspoon nutmeg
1 teaspoon cloves
1 cup solid white vegetable shortening
1 cup sugar
1¼ cup unsulphured molasses (use robust molasses for dark gingerbread)
2 eggs, beaten

Thoroughly blend flour, soda, salt and spices; set aside. Melt shortening in large saucepan. Add sugar, molasses and eggs; mix well. When mixture is cool, add 4 cups of the blended dry ingredients and mix well. Preheat oven to 350°F or temp. specified. Spray cookie sheets with vegetable-oil pan spray or grease with vegetable shortening.

Turn mixture onto light floured surface. Knead in remaining dry ingredients by hand. Add a little more flour, if necessary, to make a firm dough.

Roll out dough on lightly oiled cookie sheets. (Wilton cookie sheets have no edges and will not buckle during baking, making them a smart investment.) Baking time varies according to thickness of rolled dough. For large pieces, ⅛-¼″ thick, bake as long as 17-20 minutes. For smaller pieces, rolled thinly, 6 to 15 minutes may be enough. Check frequently to avoid over-browning. Remove from cookie sheets to wire racks with a large spatula. Cool about 30 minutes. Cover flat surface, counter or cookie sheet, with paper toweling and place baked pieces on it to dry and crisp overnight.

To store, wrap dough tightly in plastic wrap and refrigerate. Knead briefly to roll out. Yields enough for most of our projects. If additional dough is needed, it will be noted. When making a project with sides that fit together, lean them together to make sure that they fit. Cut away excess or trim to fit with a craft knife.

Eye-poppin' Teddy Garland

*It's fun to string along a darling troop of dancin' cookie
bears between popcorn "clouds." Invite them to trim the tree,
encircle a wreath or warm the hearth.*

You'll need
- Teddy Bear Cookie Mold
- Decorating Tips 2, 13
- Christmas Red, Kelly Green Icing Colors
- Grandma's Gingerbread Recipe (p. 32)
- Royal Icing Recipe (p. 6)
- Regular or tinted popcorn for stringing; red and green ⅛ in. satin ribbon, cotton kitchen twine

Step I—make bear cookies
Prepare dough according to recipe.
Using stand up bear mold, press dough
into mold; lay 9 in. length of string across
dough at back of arms; cover string with
a little piece of dough. Press firmly to
seal in string. Bake according to recipe
directions. Remove carefully. Allow to
cool completely.

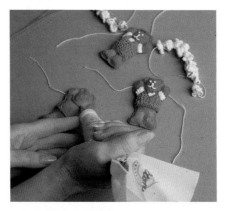

Step II—for popcorn
String 4 in. of popcorn in the middle of a
10 in. strand of twine leaving 3 in. of
string on each end.

Step III—trim the bears
Decorate cooled cookies with royal icing.
Outline outfits and faces with tip 2. Fill in
clothes with tip 13 stars. Let dry.

Step IV—tying the Knots
Alternate bears and popcorn strands,
tying strings together with knot close
to each bear, then cut off excess string
close to knot. Add a ribbon bow to cover
the knot on each side of the bear.

Stained Glass Tudor Village

*The glow of light pouring through the colorful candy windows
of these charming gingerbread facades will brighten spirits.
What a sparkling touch to add to the mantel or
surround the Christmas tree.*

You'll need
- Cookie Sheets
- Decorating Tip 47
- Christmas Red, Kelly Green, Lemon Yellow Icing Colors
- Light (2 recipes) & Dark (½ recipe) Grandma's Gingerbread (p. 32)
- Stained Glass Candy Recipe (this page)

Step I—make & bake house pieces
Grease cookie sheets and roll out dough to ¼ in. thickness. Transfer pattern piece as described on p. 80. Using Facade Patterns, p. 72-74, cut A & B patterns, chimney (optional), eaves and stand for smaller houses. For large house, cut front and roof with pattern C. Extend eaves pattern ¾ in. on each end. Use the round end of tip 47 to cut roof tiles out. Cover roof, working in rows from bottom to top, overlapping to add dimension. Add shutters to window. Add detail (bricks, woodworking and slats of shutters) by scoring surface of dough with a sharp knife.

To dark gingerbread, add one egg to make a consistency that can be piped. Fit decorating bag with tip 47 and fill with dough. Outline (before piece is baked) tudor trim with ribbed stripes. Bake pieces for 15 minutes. Remove and cool on racks.

Step II—add stained glass & stands
Cover back of cookie sheet with aluminum. If you wish, mark the size of the windows, but remember that candy

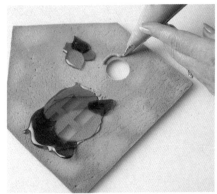

should flow over lines. Follow directions in recipe. Attach windows and stands to back of gingerbread with royal icing.

Stained Glass (Hard) Candy Recipe
2 cups granulated sugar
⅔ cup water
¼ teaspoon cream of tartar
Icing Color
1 teaspoon candy flavor
candy thermometer

Combine water, sugar and cream of tartar in heavy saucepan and bring to a boil over high heat, stirring constantly. When it begins to boil, insert candy thermometer and stop stirring. Continue cooking over high heat, occasionally wiping sides of pan and thermometer with wet pastry brush. It will take 12 to 15 minutes for candy to cook, but check thermometer often. When candy reaches 300° remove from heat. Let stand a minute or two until bubbles disappear. Stir in icing color and flavoring.

To create stained glass: Cover work surface with a large sheet of lightly oiled aluminum foil. Pour candy mixture into small metal measuring cups (they can be heated if candy starts to harden). Tint desired colors. Pour each color (be sure they touch) onto foil. Let set at room temperature to harden.

For molding hard candy: Spray hard candy molds with non-stick vegetable oil spray. Pour candy into molds and let harden at room temperature (do not refrigerate). Note: Hard candy can only be molded in hard candy molds (opaque in color).

Cozy Stone Cottage

*Quaint, charming and fun to build. Roll the stones out of
gingerbread (the kids will love helping). Shingle the roof
with pieces of chewing gum. Warm the scene with a billow of
cotton smoke. Top it off with fluffy drifts of icing "snow."*

You'll need
- Cookie Sheets
- Gingerbread House Kit
- Brown, Kelly Green, Wilton Red
  Icing Colors
- Decorating Tips 2, 3, 13, 21
- 16 In. Cake Circles, Fanci-Foil Wrap
- Grandma's Gingerbread (p. 32)
  2 recipes needed
- Royal Icing Recipe (p. 6)
- Cinnamon-flavor chewing gum
  (17 sticks needed)
- Red cinnamon candy, striped candy
  sticks (6 needed), candy-coated
  chocolates
- Sugar ice cream cone, marshmallow
- Large cotton ball

Step I—make, cut, roll & bake gingerbread

Use the Cozy Cottage patterns included
in the Gingerbread House Kit (excluding
dormer). The dormer (cut 2 of each
piece), chimney, windows and door patterns are on p. 75. On one side wall, cut
out round window (1¼ in. from peak);
on front wall cut out door and window.
Remove door piece and bake separately.

For stones: Roll remaining dough into ½
in. diameter logs. Cut into ¼ in. pieces.
Roll pieces into balls to cover front, back
and side walls of house and each side of
chimney. Press balls onto dough so each
one touches; flatten slightly. Leave ⅛ in.
at the top of each house piece uncovered
so that the roof will fit properly. Hint:
Arrange "stones" around the outer
edges, window and door openings first,
then fill in the remaining area in a random
pattern. Bake and cool.

Step II—assemble

Double cake circles and cover with

Fanci-Foil Wrap (see p. 80). Mark base
where walls will go. Cover marks with tip
21 brown tinted icing. Push the back wall
onto icing line. Pipe icing on each edge;
attach side walls, then front. Support
walls with a heavy jar or can. Let dry
until hard.

On waxed paper, attach dormer and
chimney pieces together with icing.
Note: Let dormers dry with side A
on work surface.

To tile roof: Cut cinnamon gum sticks
into 3rds. Dot each piece or ice small
areas of roof at a time (if icing is too
thick, it will ooze out). Work in rows,
overlapping slightly, from bottom up.

Attach dormers to roof. Cover roofs
with "tiles." Attach eaves to dormers;
chimney and door to house.

Step III—decorate

Decorate tree and bush on a piece of
waxed paper. For tree: Starting at the
base of sugar cone, cover with tip 16
pull-out stars (work in circular rows). For
bush: Cover in the same manner. Trim
both with cinnamon candy. Let dry.

Outline door and add knob with tip 3.
Pipe tip 13 pull-out star wreath. Trim
with tip 2 berries and bow. Attach candy
sticks to chimney and walls. Cover top of
chimney, roof and cake circle with icing
"snow" (to make icing fluffier, add 1
teaspoon corn syrup to each cup). Pat
and fluff to resemble drifting snow.
Peaked drifts on roof can be piped
with a tip 3.

Cover path with cinnamon candies and
edge cake circle with candy-coated
chocolates. Position tree and bush. Pull
out cotton ball and place in chimney.

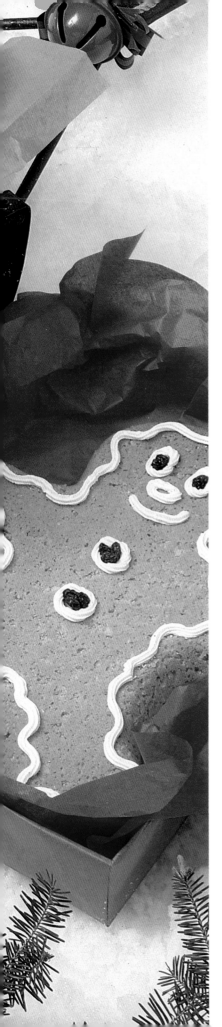

Colossal Pan Cookies

Enormously appealing, especially with children. Let them get into the act by pressing the cookie dough into the pan and decorating after the cookie is cool.

You'll need
- Rudy Reindeer, Shining Star, Gingerbread Boy Pans
- Decorating Tips 3, 16
- Wilton Red, Kelly Green, Brown Icing Colors
- Chocolate Cookie Recipe (below) for Rudy Reindeer cookie. Use favorite oatmeal (Gingerbread Boy) or chocolate chip (Star) cookie dough recipe that yields 2 to 3 dozen cookies
- Royal Icing Recipe (p. 6)

Chocolate Cookie Recipe
¾ cup butter or margarine
¾ cup sugar
2 large eggs
1 teaspoon vanilla
2¾ cups flour
2 teaspoons baking powder
⅓ cup unsweetened cocoa powder

Preheat oven to 400°F. Cream butter and sugar. Beat in eggs and vanilla. Add flour, baking powder and cocoa, one cup at a time, mixing well after each addition. The dough will be very stiff and it may be necessary to blend the last flour in by hand. Do not chill dough.

A double batch of cookie dough can be made, if a heavy mixer is used.

Step I—make, mold & bake cookie dough
Grease and dust Rudy Reindeer Pan with unsweetened cocoa powder. Preheat oven to 375°F. Carefully press dough into bottom of prepared pan, starting at the top and working down to eliminate air bubbles. Bake for 17 to 20 minutes or until edges begin to pull away from the pan. Turn out onto a rack to cool.

We used a recipe which yields 3 dozen cookies for Oatmeal Gingerbread Boy. He was baked at 400°F for 20 to 25 minutes. For the Star, we prepared two 28 oz. chocolate chip cookie mixes according to package directions and baked 20 to 25 minutes.

Step II—decorate
Rudy: Outline bow, antlers and eyes with tip 3; face and area around eye with tip 16. Pipe in eye with tip 3. Cover antlers and bow with tip 16 stars. Attach candy nose.

Gingerbread Boy: Use tip 16 for all decorating. Add raisin "button."

Star: Fill an uncut disposable decorating bag half full of Candy Melts™ or chocolate chips. Microwave 1 minute at half power; squeeze bag. Repeat at 30-second intervals until candy is completely melted. Then cut the end off bag and drizzle on corners and around edge. Let set.

Away In a Manger

Create this symbolic scene to give joy and meaning to your holiday season. Sugar ice cream cones are transformed into the holy couple, angels and wisemen. The decorating is easy enough for children to do! Pipe a thatched icing roof on the gingerbread manger and cover the floor with toasted coconut "straw" for a realistic look.

You'll need
- Cookie Sheets
- Star Cutter Set
- Gingerbread Cutter Set
- Rectangle Cake Boards, Fanci-Foil Wrap
- Brown, Golden Yellow, Royal Blue, Wilton Red, Kelly Green Icing Colors
- Decorating Tips 2, 2B, 3, 5, 8, 14, 16, 17, 21, 86, 104, 233
- Grandma's Gingerbread Recipe (p. 32)
- Royal Icing Recipe (p. 6)
- Sugar Ice cream cones (6 needed)
- Pretzel rods (12 needed)
- Pretzel sticks (7 needed)
- Candy discs, open-center hard candies
- 3 cups toasted coconut
- Sugar cubes

Step I—make patterns, cut & bake gingerbread

Transfer pattern pieces as described on p. 80. Cut out creche and manger pieces (p. 77-79); use 2 in star and gingerbread boy cutter for star and infant. Bake and cool.

Cover rectangle cake board with Fanci-Foil (see p. 80).

Step II—assemble creche and manger

Mark guidelines where walls will go on your cake board. Cover lines with tip 21 brown royal icing to hold the sides as you assemble the creche. Stand the back wall first; attach the side and front walls by piping brown icing along each seam. The side walls should be butted into the front and back wall. Place a can or jar on sides to hold walls in position. Attach the front of the creche last. Let the icing set until hard.

When walls are set, pipe icing around the top edge of the walls. Add roof panels

and let dry overnight. Attach pieces of manger together and let dry.

Step III—decorate figures

For Figures: Thin royal icing slightly for icing areas on cones smooth. Let set before adding additional decorations. "Paint" face areas on cones and cookie with thinned royal icing (tint with a very small amount of brown icing color). Let dry. Candy discs are used for "halos;" open-centered hard candies for crowns; sugar cubes are gifts. Attach all with dots of icing as indicated below.

Mary: Ice robe area blue. Pipe tip 2B smooth stripe down front. Edge neck and robe with tip 2 zigzags. With heavy pressure, squeeze out arms with tip 8.

Pipe tip 14 stripe strands of hair. Add tip 104 stripe veil. Position "halo." Add facial features with tip 2. Pipe tip 3 dot hands.

Joseph: Ice robe brown. Figure pipe tip 8 arms. Add tip 2 facial features, fingers and sash. Pipe tip 14 hair, beard and mustache. Position "halo."

Wisemen: Ice front of one cone smooth. Cover robes with tip 17 elongated zigzags (vary directions for a different look) and stars. Trim edges of robes with tip 17 zigzags or tip 86 ruffles. Figure pipe arms with tip 17. Edge sleeves with tip 14 zigzags. Position "gifts." Pipe tip 2 facial features, fingers, necklaces and ribbons on gifts. Add tip 14 stripe strands of hair and mustache. Position crowns and trim with tip 2 zigzags.

Angel: Place waxed paper over Wings Pattern (p. 79) and outline with tip 5. Let dry. Ice cone white. Figure pipe tip 8 arms. Trim neck, sleeves and hems; add dot hands and facial features with tip 2. Pipe tip 14 shell-motion curls. Position "halo." Attach wings with dots of icing.

For creche: Attach pretzel rods around sides, sticks around doorway. Cover roof with tip 233 pull-out strands of straw. Work from bottom of the roof towards the peak. Outline star cookie with tip 3. Add tip 16 scrolls. Let dry. Attach to peak with dots of icing.

For manger: Pipe tip 233 pull-out strands of hay. Ice infant's face smooth. Outline body and facial features with tip 2. Cover body with tip 14 stars. Attach candy disc "halo."

Ice cake board with brown-tinted icing. Pat with toasted coconut. Position manger, infant, holy couple, angel and wisemen.

Candy, Breads & Desserts

Tree Of Joy

Mold a festive 3-D tree out of Candy Melts and trim with candy ornaments. It's a treat for all eyes.

You'll need
- Holiday Tree Pan Kit
- Candy Melts™*–3 bags Green; 1 each Christmas Mix, Dark Cocoa, White
- Candy Molds–Bells, Christmas Classics, Christmas II
- Tuk 'n Ruffle
- Decorator's Brush

Step I–mold tree
Pour approximately 1½ bags of coating into each tree pan half. Rotate pans to coat areas. Refrigerate for 10 minutes, then rotate pan again. Repeat procedure until all coating sets. While candy sets,

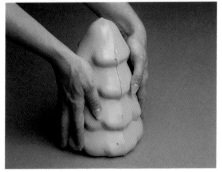

trim serving tray with white Tuk 'n Ruffle. Unmold tree halves onto hand or soft towels (tap pan, if necessary). To attach together, run the edges over a warm hot tray or cookie sheet. Immediately push halves together. Place on serving tray.

Step II–make candy ornaments
Use a decorator's brush dipped in melted Candy Melts. Paint features or details desired. Refrigerate until partially set. Fill mold. Refrigerate until set. Unmold. Attach to tree with dots of melted coating.

Candy Cottages

Oh fudge! Everyone loves it. We shaped it in the Holiday House Pan, then added charming molded trims. Try our delicious recipes, or use your favorite.

You'll need
- Holiday House Pan
- Disposable Decorating Bags
- Candy Melts™–Christmas Mix, White, Light & Dark Cocoa
- Penuche, White Peppermint Fudge, Cocoa Fudge Recipes

White Peppermint Fudge Recipe
14 oz. package (3 cups) White Candy Melts
1 can (14 ounces) sweetened condensed milk, (not evaporated)
½ cup marshmallows creme
½ cup coarsely chopped peppermint candy
1 teaspoon clear vanilla

In a heavy 2-quart saucepan, melt Candy Melts with milk; stir constantly.

Remove from heat; add marshmallow creme, peppermint candy and vanilla; stir until melted. Pour into buttered Holiday House Pan. Refrigerate until firm, about 2 hours. Remove from pan.

Penuche Recipe
This no-beat confectionery coating fudge has a rich caramel flavor and delicate grain.
1½ cups granulated sugar
¾ cup light brown sugar, lightly packed
1 Tablespoon light corn syrup
1½ cups whipping cream
4 Tablespoon butter
½ cup (2¼ ounces) white Candy Melts

Butter sides of a heavy 4-quart saucepan and Holiday House Pan. Place sugars, syrup and cream in saucepan. Place over medium heat and stir constantly with a wooden spoon until all sugar crystals are dissolved. Continue cooking, stirring occasionally. When thermometer registers 237°F (softball stage) remove from heat. Total cooking time is about 30 minutes.

Allow to stand, undisturbed, about 10 minutes. While mixture is standing, cut butter into thin slices and place on surface to melt–do not stir.

Add Candy Melts and stir thoroughly until coating is melted, butter is incorporated and mixture thickens. Press into buttered Holiday House pan, using a rubber scraper. Refrigerate about 40 minutes until firm.

Ready-In-Minutes Cocoa Fudge Recipe
20 ounces (approximately 4¼ cups) Dark Cocoa Candy Melts
1 (14 ounce) can condensed milk (not evaporated)

Melt wafers on low power in microwave-safe container. Add milk; stir until blended. Microwave an additional 2 to 3 minutes on medium power; stir until fudge develops a sheen.

Pour mixture into buttered Holiday House Pan and refrigerate until set.

To decorate:
When cold and firmly set, remove candy from pan by running a spatula or table knife around edges, gently lifting candy. If difficult to remove, place a dampened, warm towel over pan. Set aside.

Melt Candy Melts in disposable decorating bags following microwave directions on package. Snip the end off bag and fill in the door, shutters and eaves indentations inside the Holiday House Pan. Place in freezer for 2 to 3 minutes to set. Unmold. Attach pieces to houses with dots of melted coating. Trim eaves and outline windows with melted coating by using a cut bag or, for more control, tape decorating tip 2 over opening. Let set.

Lollipop Go-Round

*Mold classic marshmallow crisp rice cereal treats into
a centerpiece show-stopper!*

You'll need
- 8 in. Ring Mold
- Holiday Lollipop Molds
- Red & Green Candy Colors
- Candy Flavor (optional)
- Lollipop Sticks & Bags
- Wide and narrow satin ribbons
- Hard Candy Recipe (p. 37)

Prepare marshmallow crisp rice cereal treat recipe according to directions on cereal box. Spray pan with pan spray. Pack mixture into pan and let set.

Spray Holiday Lollipop Molds with non-stick vegetable oil spray. Using hard candy recipe, mold lollipops. Make extras to give away. (Recipe will yield about 10.) Protect with our Lollipop Bags and tie up in ribbon.

Unmold ring by placing a serving plate on top of mold and turning over. Remove pan. Place ribbon and bow around sides. Push in lollipops.

Change-Of-Taste Pops
Chewy and delicious, these treats are sure to go over big.

For either recipe you'll need
- Holiday Lollipop Molds
- Lollipop Sticks & Bags
- Candy Melts™

Cocoa Raisin Pops
1½ cups (7 ounces) Wilton Dark Cocoa
Candy Melts™
½ cup raisins, chopped
3 Tablespoons
chopped unsalted peanuts
½ teaspoon vanilla

Place Candy Melts in 4-cup glass measuring cup. Microwave at HIGH 1 to 2 minutes or until almost melted, stirring twice. Stir until smooth. Stir in raisins, peanuts and vanilla. Immediately press Candy Melt mixture into lollipop molds; add lollipop sticks. Refrigerate until firm; unmold.

Makes 10 candies

Peanut Butterscotch Pops
½ cup peanut butter chips
½ cup butterscotch chips
1 teaspoon peanut butter
3 cups crisp rice cereal
2 Tablespoons
chopped unsalted peanuts
For variation: (see below)
1 cup (6 ounces) of any
color Candy Melt

Combine chips and peanut butter in 4-cup glass measuring cup. Microwave at HIGH 1 to 2 minutes or until almost melted, stirring twice. Stir until smooth. Add cereal and peanuts.

Immediately press about 1 Tablespoon of mixture into lollipop molds; add lollipop sticks. Refrigerate until firm; unmold.

Variation: Place 1 teaspoon of melted Candy Melts into each mold and tap on table to coat evenly. Place molded Change-of-Taste lollipops into mold sections and refrigerate until firm. Unmold and trim edges with a sharp knife.

Makes 10 treats.

Crescent Coffee Cakes

Shape ready-made dough into a tree or a star for breakfast, brunch or midnight noshing. The nut glaze on the tree cake is added before baking to seal in freshness and make it glisten. Will serve a few or many, depending on the occasion.

You'll need
• Treelightful (or Star) Pan
• Decorating Tip 16 (or Tips 2B, 47)

Crescent Coffee Cake Recipe
3 packages (8 ounces each)
refrigerator crescent rolls
6 Tablespoons brown sugar
6 Tablespoons granulated sugar
1½ teaspoons cinnamon
6 Tablespoons raisins

Nut Glaze:
(for bottom of pan)
¼ cup butter, divided
¼ cup brown sugar
1 Tablespoon light corn syrup
¼ cup chopped pecans

Preheat oven to 375°F.
For Treelightful coffee cake, divide dough from each package into 2 rectangles. Press perforations together to form 4 x 12 in. rectangles.

Combine sugars, cinnamon, and raisins in a small bowl. Sprinkle sugar mixture evenly over dough rectangles, leaving one long edge plain.

Starting with the widest edge, roll up and press plain edge to seal roll. Cut into 1″ pieces. Hint: To cut, slide a strong thread or string under dough. Bring ends up and twist together tightly. This prevents flattening dough as a knife would.

For nut glaze, melt 1 Tablespoon butter and brush bottom and sides of Treelightful Pan. Heat remaining butter, sugar and syrup until melted; stirring to combine. Pour mixture evenly into prepared pan; sprinkle with pecans.

Place 1″ pieces of dough (cut edges down) into pan filling in all spaces. Bake at 375°F for 20 to 25 minutes or until golden brown. Invert onto serving platter.

To decorate: Use tip 16 and buttercream icing to add a garland across the tree and stars at random. Top with a maraschino cherry.

Variation: To make this recipe in the Shining Star Pan, use an additional package of crescent rolls and omit the nut glaze. With buttercream icing and tip 2B, pipe a wide smooth band 1 in. from edge of cake. Edge with tip 47 ribbed stripes. Alternate red and green cherry halves.

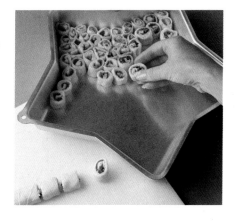

Frosty Mousse Snowman

Unmolding this chilly dilly is such a thrill. He's a light-as-air delight that can be whipped up in no time at all. Serves 10.

You'll need
- Stand-Up Snowman Pan
- Decorating Tips 8, 21
- White Candy Melts™

White Mousse Recipe
⅔ cup (4 ounces) White Candy Melts
4 eggs, separated
½ cup confectioners sugar
1 (1.4 ounce) envelope whipped topping mix

Cocoa Cream Topping:
½ cup whipping cream
2 teaspoons unsweetened cocoa powder

Melt white Candy Melts in double boiler, stirring constantly until smooth. Turn off heat and let stand over warm water. Prepare whipped topping according to package directions.

Beat egg yolks and sugar with electric mixer in large bowl. Slowly beat in white Candy Melts mixture.

In separate bowl with clean beaters, beat egg whites until soft peaks form. Fold egg whites gently into white Candy Melts mixture. Fold in whipped topping.

Line Snowman Pan with plastic wrap. Pour mousse mixture into pan; cover with foil. Freeze 6 hours or overnight until firm. Carefully pull plastic wrap to unmold onto serving platter.

For Cocoa Cream Topping, combine ½ cup whipping cream with cocoa, whip to stiff peaks. Or if you wish, use 1 envelope of topping mix, add cocoa to dry mix and prepare, following package directions. You'll have extra topping to serve with mousse. To decorate with cocoa cream, use tip 8 for face and tip 21 for scarf.

Stabilized Whipped Cream Icing
We recommend stabilizing whipped cream when you want decorations to hold up longer.
1 tsp. unflavored gelatin
4 tsps. cold water
1 cup heavy whipping cream (at least 24 hours old and very cold)
¼ cup confectioners sugar
½ tsp. Clear Vanilla Extract

Combine gelatin and cold water in small saucepan. Let stand until thick. Place over low heat, stirring constantly just until gelatin dissolves. Remove from heat and cool slightly. Whip cream, sugar, and vanilla until slightly thickened. While beating slowly, gradually add gelatin to whipped cream mixture. Whip at high speed until stiff. Makes 2 cups.

Raspberry Mousse Tree

This merry berry "treeat" can be whipped up in no time, too! It's so delicious, everyone will want the recipe. Serves 10 guests.

You'll need
- Holiday Tree Cake Pan
- Decorating Tip 2A

Frozen Raspberry Mousse Recipe
2 envelopes unflavored gelatin
½ cup cold water
2 packages (10 ounces each) frozen raspberries, defrosted
2 cups non-dairy whipped topping

Soften gelatin in water in small saucepan. Place over low heat; stir until dissolved.

Spray Holiday Tree Cake Pan with non-stick vegetable spray.

In blender or food processor process raspberries until smooth; strain out seeds. Stir strained raspberries into dissolved gelatin. Allow to thicken slightly. Fold in whipped topping.

Pour into pan; tap pan firmly against counter several times to remove excess air bubbles. Cover with foil. Freeze for 2 to 4 hours or until firm.

Loosen sides with spatula and unmold onto serving platter. Decorate with whipped topping and tip 2A.

Note: To defrost raspberries in microwave oven, remove metal top and bottom from raspberry packages. Place in glass baking dish. Microwave at 30% power for 4 to 5 minutes; rotate ¼ turn halfway through defrosting.

Molded Marvels

*You'll have a craving for these light and luscious desserts the
year 'round. Use different shaped pans to suit the occasion.
For Christmas, a gingerbread boy, petite rings and mini trees
look right at home.*

Apricot Nectar Gingerbread Boy
Serves 8.

You'll need
- Gingerbread Boy Pan
- Decorating Tip 21
- Raisins
- Whipped Cream

3 envelopes unflavored gelatin
½ cup cold water
3½ cups apricot nectar

Soften gelatin in cold water in a medium
saucepan. Place over low heat and stir
until dissolved. Stir in apricot nectar. Pour
mixture into Gingerbread Boy Pan and
chill until firm.

To unmold, dip pan into warm water only
10 to 15 seconds. Place serving dish over
mold and invert. Note: If gelatin does not
unmold after dipping pan in warm water,
use hot, damp towel around mold to
soften further.

With whipped cream and tip 21, outline
vest, bow tie, and buttons. Trim with
raisins.

Glistening Ring Molds
You'll need
- Fancy Petite Ring Molds
- Leaf Green Icing Color

Honey Yogurt Cream Recipe
4 ½ teaspoons unflavored gelatin
(1½ envelopes)
½ cup cold water
3 cartons (8 ounces each)
lemon flavored yogurt
½ cup honey
1½ cups whipping cream, whipped
until it holds a shape, not dry
Lime slices
Cherry halves
Lettuce leaves

Soften gelatin in water in small saucepan.
Place over low heat and stir until dissolved. Combine yogurt and honey in
a large bowl. Gradually add dissolved
gelatin; mix well. If desired, stir in green
icing color, a small amount at a time until
desired color is reached. Chill about 5
minutes or until slightly thickened. Fold
in whipped cream.

Spray Fancy Petite Ring Molds with
non-stick vegetable spray. Pour yogurt
mixture into prepared molds. Refrigerate
at least 4 hours or until set.

Unmold onto lettuce leaves. Arrange
lime slices and cherry halves around base.

Creamy Christmas Trees
Each recipe makes 6 servings.

You'll need
- Mini Christmas Tree Pan
- Decorating Tip 18
- Leaf Green Icing Color
- Creme de Menthe Candy Flavor
- Grasshopper Pie & Strawberry Creme
  Recipes
- Whipped Cream

Grasshopper Pie Recipe
1 envelope unflavored gelatin
½ cup cold water
½ teaspoon Creme de Menthe candy
flavor
1 Tablespoon white Creme de Cacao
liqueur
1 jar (7 ounces) marshmallow creme
½ cup whipping cream, whipped until
it holds a shape, not dry
¾ cup chocolate cookie crumbs (about 20
chocolate wafer cookies)
¼ cup butter or margarine, melted
Whipped cream for decorating

Soften gelatin in water in small saucepan. Place over low heat and stir until
dissolved. Beat liqueur and candy flavor
into marshmallow creme. Gradually
add dissolved gelatin; mix well. Chill about
15 minutes or until slightly thickened.
Fold in whipped cream.

Spray Mini Christmas Tree Pan with
non-stick vegetable spray. Pour gelatin
mixture into prepared molds, leaving
¼-inch space at top. Combine crumbs
and butter in small bowl. Layer crumb
mixture on top of filling; press gently. Refrigerate at least 4 hours or until set.

Unmold by dipping quickly in warm water,
then loosening sides with a small knife or
spatula. Decorate with whipped cream
stars, using tip 18.

Strawberry Creme Recipe
1 envelope unflavored gelatin
½ cup cold water
1 package (10 ounces) frozen
strawberries in light syrup, thawed
1 cup non-dairy whipped topping
1 cup vanilla sandwich cookie crumbs
(about 10 cookies)
3 Tablespoons butter or margarine,
melted

Soften gelatin in water in small saucepan.
Place over low heat and stir until dissolved. Stir strawberries into dissolved
gelatin; mix well. Chill about 5 minutes or
until slightly thickened. Fold in
whipped topping.

Spray Mini Christmas Tree Pan with
non-stick vegetable spray. Pour strawberry mixture into prepared molds,
leaving ¼ in. space at top.

Combine crumbs and melted butter in
small bowl. Layer crumb mixture on top
of filling; press gently. Refrigerate at least
4 hours or until set. Unmold by dipping
quickly in warm water or by loosening
with a small knife or spatula. Decorate
with tip 18 whipped cream stars.

Present-Perfect Mini Breads

Little loaves tied up with icing ribbons will have enormous appeal. Ideal for serving, gifting and selling at bake sales. Each recipe yields 6 to 8 loaves.

You'll need
- Mini Loaf Pan Set
- Decorating Tips 17, 47, 102
- Wilton Red, Leaf Green Icing Colors
- Banana Nut Bread Recipe
- Cranberry Orange Bread Recipe
- Royal Icing Recipe, p. 6

Banana Nut Bread Recipe
⅓ cup butter or margarine
⅔ cup sugar
½ teaspoon grated lemon peel
2 eggs, beaten
1½ cups mashed ripe bananas (about 3 medium size)
1¾ cups flour
2 teaspoons baking pwder
½ teaspoon salt
½ cup coarsely chopped walnuts or pecans

Preheat oven to 350°F. Cream butter and sugar in large bowl until light and fluffy; stir in lemon peel. Stir in eggs and bananas. Combine flour, baking powder and salt. Add to banana mixture slowly; stir just until moistened. Fold in nuts.

Grease and flour Mini Loaf Pan Set. Pour scant ½ cup of batter into each pan. Bake at 350°F for 30 to 35 minutes or until wooden pick inserted in center comes out clean.

Cool on rack. Glaze or decorate.

Brown Sugar Glaze
3 Tablespoons butter or margarine
⅓ cup brown sugar
3 Tablespoons whipping cream
½ teaspoon vanilla

Combine butter, sugar and cream in saucepan. Bring to a boil over medium heat. Let boil 1 minute.

Remove from heat; stir in vanilla. Spoon or pour over cooled loaves.

Cranberry Orange Bread Recipe
½ cup butter or margarine
1 cup sugar
2 eggs
½ cup milk
2 cups flour
2 teaspoons baking powder
½ teaspoon salt
1 cup fresh or frozen cranberries, coarsely chopped
1½ teaspoons grated orange peel
½ cup coarsely chopped pecans

Preheat oven to 375°F. Cream butter and sugar until light and fluffy. Beat in eggs, one at a time; add milk. Combine flour, baking powder, and salt. Add to butter mixture; stir just until moistened. Fold cranberries, orange peel, and pecans into batter.

Grease and flour Mini Loaf Pan Set. Pour ½ cup batter into each pan. Bake at 375°F for 25 to 30 minutes or until wooden pick inserted in center comes out clean. Cool on rack. Glaze or decorate.

Orange Glaze
1 cup confectioners sugar
1 Tablespoon plus 1 teaspoon orange juice

Combine confectioners sugar and orange juice in a small bowl; stir. Drizzle over each Cranberry Orange Bread.

To Decorate: Pipe ribbon bows and streamers with red and green royal icing. Use tips 16, 47 or 102. Let icing dry, then wrap loosely in foil or plastic wrap.

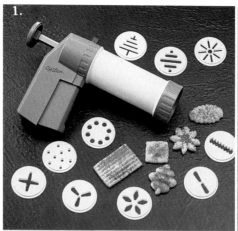

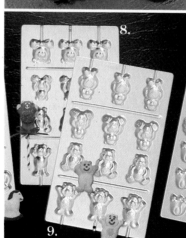

1. SPRITZ COOKIE PRESS
Ideal for making delicious cookies to fill the gingerbread bowl on p. 31 or our cookie box Santa p. 32. Easy-squeeze trigger-action makes it fun to create these rich, buttery delights–try our kitchen-tested recipe. 10 plastic disks let you bake fancy classic and favorite holiday cookie shapes. Gray/white plastic. **2104-2303**

2. GINGERBREAD FAMILY SET
Classic favorites–mom, dad and the kids are always a joy to have around. Set includes two 5½ x 4 in. adults and two 2½ x 1½ in. children. **2304-121**

3. 10-PC. CHRISTMAS CUTTER SET
Sturdy plastic canister contains 9 festive cutters. Canister is great for storing cookies, too! **509-1225**

4. HOLIDAY SHAPES SET
Tie with ribbons and use as tree trimmers. Santa, angel, tree, boy and girl–3⅝ to 6 in. high. **2304-105**

5. CHRISTMAS CUTTERS
Super size–perfect for munching. See an array in the holly tray on p. 30.
COTTAGE 509-1221
HOLLY 509-1222
REINDEER 509-1223
SNOWMAN 509-1224

6. 6-PC. STAR SET
Used on the sides of glowing luminarias, p. 23. From 1⅝ to 4⅝ in. **2304-111**

7. 6-PC. OVAL SET
One of the most elegant, yet difficult shapes to duplicate. Great to mark cakes with, too. From 3¼ tp 7 in. long–2⅛ to 4¾ in. wide. **2304-388**

8-9 COOKIE MOLDS
Just press in dough, add string and bake to make a garland of dancing teddies that deserve rave reviews. See them on p. 34. Aluminum.
8. TEDDY BEARS 2306-116
9. CARE BEARS ™ 2306-118

*© MCMLXXXVI. Those Characters From Cleveland™ designates Trademarks of Those Characters From Cleveland. Wilton Enterprises, Authorized User.

10. 6-PC. ROUND SET
The decorating possibilities are endless. Perfect for canapes, too. From 1½ to 4 in. **2304-113**

1. HEXAGON PANS
Combine geometry with artistry (see p. 30). 2 in. deep.
9 IN. 2105-5125.
12 IN. 2105-5133

2. COOKIE SHEETS
10 x 15 IN. 2105-1265
12½ x 16 IN. 2105-2975

3. RING MOLDS/PANS
Each 3 in. deep. See p. 4 for a shining example.
8 IN. 2105-190
10 IN. 2105-4013

4. 4-PC. OVAL PAN SET
Turn out a classic look for weddings and big parties. See p. 16. Set includes four 2 in. deep pans. Sizes are 7¾ x 5⅝ in.; 10¾ x 7⅞ in.; 13 x 9⅞ in.; 16 x 12⅜ in.
2105-2130

2 PC. OVAL PAN SET.
(Not shown). Used on p. 32.
2105-1553

5. MINI LOAF PAN SET
Create individual serving breads shown on p. 57. **2105-3844**

6. PETITE FANCY RING MOLDS/PANS
Diminutive desserts in elegant form. Bake six at once. Molds favorite cold desserts, too (see p. 55.) **2105-2097**

7. CAKE SAVER
Generous size accommodates borders and top decorations easily. Use to carry or store all types of cakes, including bundt, angel food, cheese cakes, even pies. Maintains freshness. Wide enough for a l0 in. cake with borders or a 12 in. cake without borders. Includes one 14 in. round base and one 6 in. high cover.
415-905

8. 9 x 13 CAKE PAN COVER
Cover, protect and transport decorated cakes in the pan. Designed for use with the Wilton 9 x 13 Performance Pan, this cover has a raised dome-like lid which allows you to cover even decorated cakes with ease. Keeps cakes and other foods fresh in the pan, even after slicing.
415-903

9. ROUND PANS...
The baking possibilities are endless. 2 in. deep.
16 IN. ROUND 2105-3963
14 IN. ROUND 2105-3947
12 IN. ROUND 2105-2215
10 IN. ROUND 2105-2207
8 IN. ROUND 2105-2193
6 IN. ROUND 2105-2185

10. SHEET PANS...
Bakes crowd-size holiday cakes (see p. 12) and main course dishes. 2 in. deep.
12 x 18 IN. SHEET 2105-182
11 x 15 IN. SHEET 2105-158
9 x 13 IN. SHEET 2105-1308
7 x 11 IN. SHEET 2105-2304

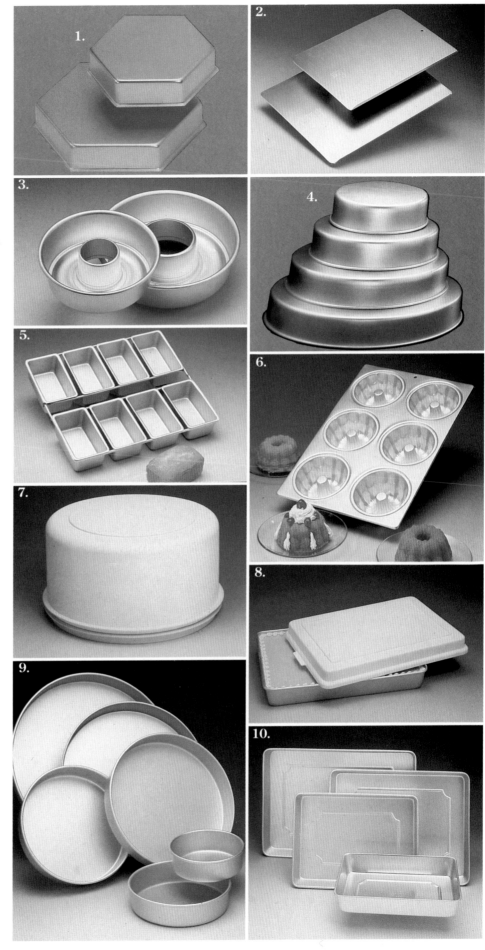

RUDY REINDEER PAN
Introducing Rudy, our irresistible reindeer: He'll soon be leading the fun at all holiday festivities. One-mix pan is 10¾ x 16¾ x 1¾ in. **2105-1224**

TREELITEFUL PAN
Here's holiday decorating made quick and easy. Just cover with one-squeeze stars, add simple garlands and candy or cookie ornaments. Instructions include several ideas for throughout the year. One-mix pan is 15 x 11 x 1½ in. **2105-425**

JOLLY SANTA PAN
Send sweet season's greetings with the smiling face of old St. Nick. He's great fun to decorate! One-mix pan is 13¼ x 11½ x 2 in. **2105-1225**

GINGERBREAD BOY PAN
Simple decorating creates great effects with this versatile pan. Cast him in all sorts of delightful roles in every season. One-mix pan is 14 x 10½ x 2 in. **2105-2072**

STAND-UP SNOWMAN PAN KIT
Here's a cheerful chap with a grin for Old Man Winter. Create a flat or 3-D cake. One-mix pan is 11½ x 6½ x 2¾ in. **2105-1394**

HUGGABLE TEDDY BEAR PAN
Now here's an old friend who's enjoying more popularity than ever. Maybe it's because he makes folks feel so good. He'll bring his happy mood to any occasion. Ideas for birthdays and baby showers included. Aluminum pan is 13½ x 12¼ x 2-in. **2105-4943**

STAR PAN

What an illustrious way to give someone the star treatment. Brighten birthdays and a galaxy of other stellar occasions. New possibilities shine through again and again with so many ways to decorate. One-mix aluminum pan is 12¾" across. **2105-2512**

HOLIDAY TREE PAN KIT

Bake a tree-trimming party treat. You have two wonderful options: A cake that lies flat or a crowd-pleasing 3-dimensional centerpiece. One-mix pan is 10½ x 3 in. **2105-1510**

MINI-CHRISTMAS TREE PAN

O Christmas trees! Lots of little ones to serve individually. Pan includes alternate ideas for year 'round versatility. 13 x 10½ x 1¼ in. **2105-1779**

GINGERBREAD HOUSE KIT

Construct a dream house in a winter wonderland. The kit includes a Tudor castle design and 3 plastic gingerbread people cutters, sturdy pattern pieces and instruction book. **2104-2946**

CHRISTMAS COOKIE TREE

Begin a new holiday tradition. Ice, stack and trim cookie stars. Kit includes 10 plastic star cutters in graduated sizes, plus instruction book. **2105-3424**

HOLIDAY HOUSE KIT

Build an enchanted cottage of cake candy and icing. One-mix pan is 8⅝ x 9 x 3 in. **2105-2282.**

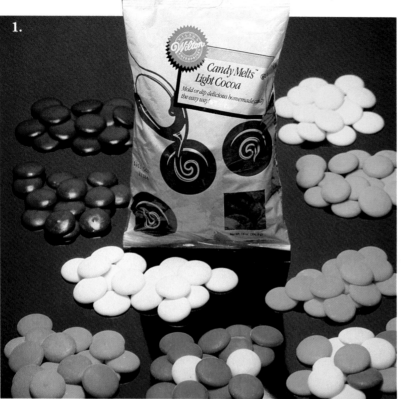

1.

1. CANDY MELTS™

Brand confectionery coating. Creamy, easy-to-melt wafers are ideal for all your candy making needs-molding, dipping and coating. Delicious taste that can be varied with our Candy Flavors. 14 oz. bag. Certified Kosher.

WHITE 1911-498
LIGHT COCOA (All natural, cocoa flavor.) **1911-544**
DARK COCOA (All natural, cocoa flavor.) **1911-358**
PINK 1911-447
YELLOW 1911-463
GREEN 1911-404
CHRISTMAS MIX (Red, Green, Yellow.) **1911-1625**

CANDY MOLDS (not shown)
For a festive selection of clear molds and opaque hard candy molds, see the current Wilton Yearbook of Cake Decorating.

2. CANDY COLORS KIT

Contains red, green, yellow, orange ¼ oz. jars.
1913-1299

CANDY COLORS (not shown)
Favorite colors in ¾ oz. jars
RED 1913-1124
YELLOW 1913-1248
GREEN 1913-1183
ORANGE 1913-1205
PINK 1913-1140

3. LOLLIPOP BAGS

Plastic bags for lollipops and other candies.
3 x 4 in. 50 bags in a pack **1912-2347.**

4. LOLLIPOP STICKS

Sturdy paper sticks are easy to add to candy molds.
4½ in. long. 50 sticks per pack. **1912-1006.**

5. STARTER CAKE DECORATING SET

• 4 metal decorating tips • Instruction booklet • Six 12-in. disposable decorating bags • Two tip couplers • Five liquid color packets.
2104-2530.

6. BASIC CAKE DECORATING SET

• 5 professional quality metal tips • Twelve 12-in. disposable bags • Two tip couplers • Flower nail no. 7 • Four ½-oz. icing colors • Instruction booklet.
2104-2536

7. DELUXE CAKE DECORATING SET

Contains 36 essentials!
• 10 nickel-plated metal tips • Four ½-oz. icing colors
• Plastic storage tray • Eighteen 12-in. disposable bags
• Two tip couplers • No. 7 flower nail • Cake Decorating, Easy As 1,2,3.
2104-2540.

8. SUPREME CAKE DECORATING SET

52 tools in all!
• 18 metal tips • Two tip couplers • Five ½-oz. icing colors
• 8-in. angled spatula • No. 9 flower nail • Twenty-four disposable 12 in. bags • Cake Decorating Easy as 1,2,3 book • Storage tray.
2104-2546.

9. DISPOSABLE DECORATING BAGS

Just use and toss-no fuss, no muss. Perfect for melting Candy Melts in the microwave, too. Strong, flexible and easy-to-handle plastic. 12 in. size fits standard tips and couplers.
2104-358 PACK OF 12   2104-1358 PACK OF 24

10. GLUCOSE

Essential ingredient for making gum paste. 24 oz. plastic jar. **707-117**

2.

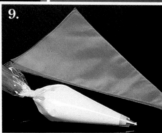

3.
4.

7.
8.
5.
6.

9.
10.

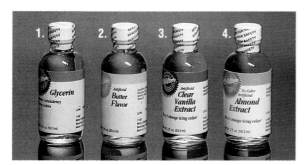

1. GLYCERIN
A few drops stirred into dried-out paste color restores consistency. 2 oz. **708-14**

2. BUTTER EXTRACT
Gives a rich, buttery taste to icing, cakes, cookies. 2 oz. **604-2040**

3. CLEAR VANILLA EXTRACT
Perfect for decorating because it won't change the color of your icing. 2 oz. Great for baking, too! **604-2237**

4. ALMOND EXTRACT
Delicious almond flavor for icing, cookies, cakes. 2 oz. **604-2126**

CREAMY WHITE ICING MIX.
Convenient mix that provides rich, homemade taste. Just add butter and milk. Ideal for frosting as well as decorating. Yields 2 cups. **710-112**

READY-TO-USE DECORATOR'S ICING.
Perfect for decorating and frosting. Use for borders, flowers, writing, etc. Just stir and use! Delicious homemade taste! 16 oz. **710-117**

MERINGUE POWDER MIX.
For royal icing, meringue, boiled icing.
8 oz. CAN. **702-6015**
4 oz. CAN. **702-6007**

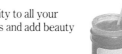

COLOR FLOW MIX
Add water and confectioners sugar for smooth icing for color flow designs. 4 oz. can yields about ten 1½ cup batches. **701-47**

PIPING GEL
Clear gel. Can be tinted with paste color. Use for glazing, writing, more. 10 oz. **704-105**

Color is vital to your decorating. With color you can add realism and vitality to all your character cakes, personalize special events cakes, highlight holiday cakes and add beauty and vibrance to all your cakes.

Wilton Icing Colors are concentrated in a rich, creamy base, are fast mixing and easy to use, and will not change your icing consistency. Our extensive range of icing colors makes it convenient for you to achieve the colors you need and want.

WILTON ICING COLORS are available in 1 oz. jars. A variety of colors is available in convenient kits.

WHITE-WHITE ICING COLOR
Just stir into icing to make icing made with butter or margarine white. Perfect for wedding cakes. 2 oz. plastic bottle. **603-1236**

DAFFODIL YELLOW 610-T-175	PINK 610-T-256	WATERMELON 610-T-353	VIOLET 610-T-604	KELLY GREEN 610-T-752
LEMON YELLOW 610-T-108	CHRISTMAS RED 610-T-302	ROSE 610-T-401	BURGUNDY 610-T-698	LEAF GREEN 610-T-809
GOLDEN YELLOW 610-T-159	RED-RED 610-T-906	COPPER 610-T-450	ROYAL BLUE 610-T-655	MOSS GREEN 610-T-851
ORANGE 610-T-205	RED (no taste) 610-T-998	BROWN 610-T-507	SKY BLUE 610-T-700	BLACK 610-T-981

10-ICING COLOR KIT
1 oz. jars of paste colors. Violet. Leaf Green, Royal Blue, Brown, Black, Pink, Watermelon, Moss Green, Orange and Lemon Yellow. **601-5569**

8-ICING COLOR KIT
½ oz. jars of paste colors. Christmas Red, Lemon Yellow, Leaf Green, Sky Blue, Brown, Orange, pink, and Violet. **601-5577**

4-COLOR ICING KIT
(SOFT PASTEL COLORS)
½ oz. jars of paste colors. Petal Pink, Creamy Peach, Willow Green, Cornflower Blue. **601-5588**

ROSE PETAL PINK†	WILLOW GREEN†
CREAMY PEACH†	CORNFLOWER BLUE†

†available in kit only.

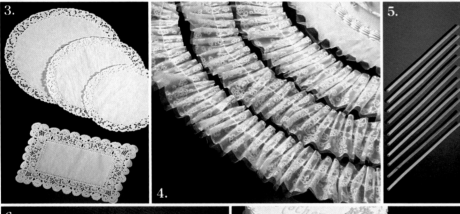

1. SHOW 'N SERVE CAKE BOARDS
Scalloped edge. Protected with grease-resistant coating. 6 in a package.
8 IN. 2104-1125
10 IN. 2104-1168
12 IN. 2104-1176
14 IN. 2104-1184
14 x 20 IN. RECTANGLE
2104-1230

2. CAKE CIRCLES & BOARD
Sturdy corrugated cardboard.

6 IN. 2104-64	**14 IN. 2104-145**
8 IN. 2104-80	**16 IN. 2104-160**
10 IN. 2104-102	**18 IN. 2104-180**
12 IN. 2104-129	
13 x 19 IN. 2104-552	

3. DOILIES
Grease-resistant, glassine-coated paper doilies are ideal for iced cakes. Round and rectangle shapes have lace borders sized to fit around your decorated cakes. Ideal for serving cookies and canapes, too!
10 IN. ROUND 2104-1310
12 IN. ROUND 2104-1312
14 IN. ROUND 2104-1314
10 x 14 IN. RECTANGLE
2104-1324

4. TUK-N-RUFFLE
Attach to serving tray or board with royal icing or tape. Order 60 ft. bolt or by the foot.

COLOR	PER FOOT
PINK	**801-708**
BLUE	**801-200**
WHITE	**801-1003**
COLOR	**60-FT. BOLT**
PINK	**802-702**
BLUE	**802-206**
WHITE	**802-1008**

5. WOODEN DOWEL RODS
Essential for supporting stacked cakes and tiers. Cut and sharpen with strong sheers and knife. 12-in. long. ¼ in. wide. Set of 12. **399-1009**

6. CAKE DIVIDING SET
Wheel chart marks 2-in. intervals on 6 to 18-in. diameter cakes. Triangle marker for precise spacing for stringwork, garlands, more. Includes instructions.
409-800

7. DECORATING COMB
Quick way to make ridges in icing. 12-in. long, plastic. **409-8259**

8. DECORATING TRIANGLE
Each side adds a different wavy effect to icing. 5 x 5-in. plastic. **409-990**

9. TREE FORMERS
Use to make icing pine trees and to dry royal icing or gum paste decorations. Set of four, 6½ in. high. **417-1150**

10. FANCI-FOIL WRAP
Serving side has a non-toxic grease-resistant surface. FDA approved for use with food. Continuous roll: 20 in x 15 ft.

ROSE 804-124	**BLUE 804-140**
GOLD 804-183	**WHITE 804-191**
SILVER 804-167	

Fantasy Forest

Script Message

Merry Christmas

Christmas Belle

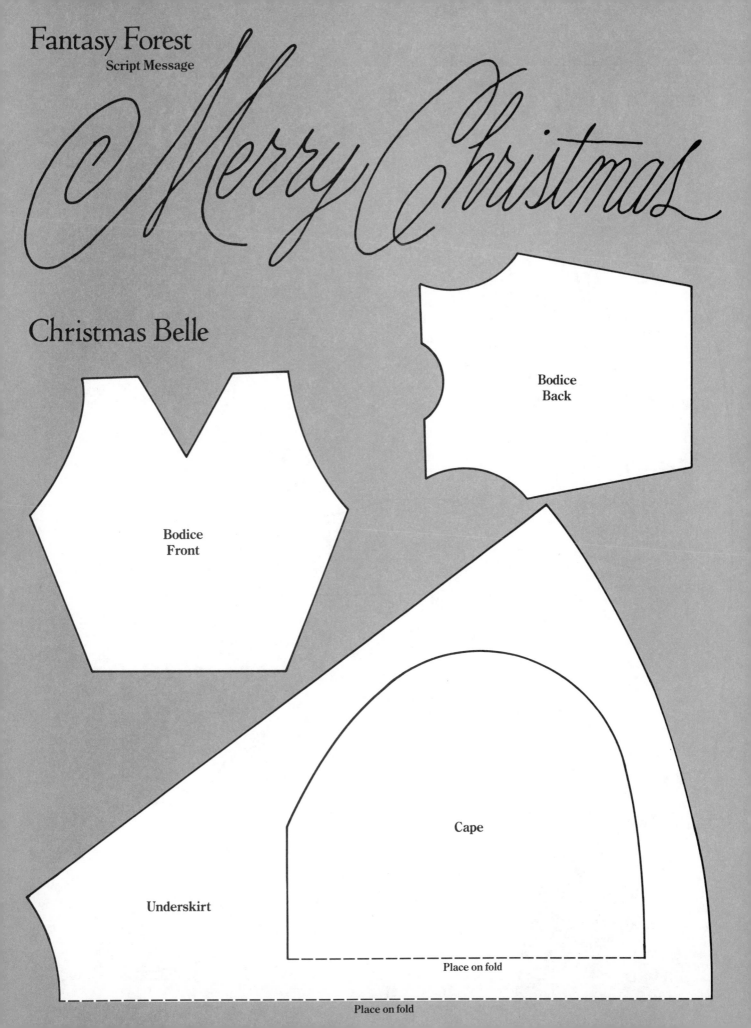

Bodice
Back

Bodice
Front

Cape

Underskirt

Place on fold

Place on fold

Christmas Belle

Fantasy Forest

Tree

Sleeve
(cut 2)

Cloak Skirt

Hood

Place on fold

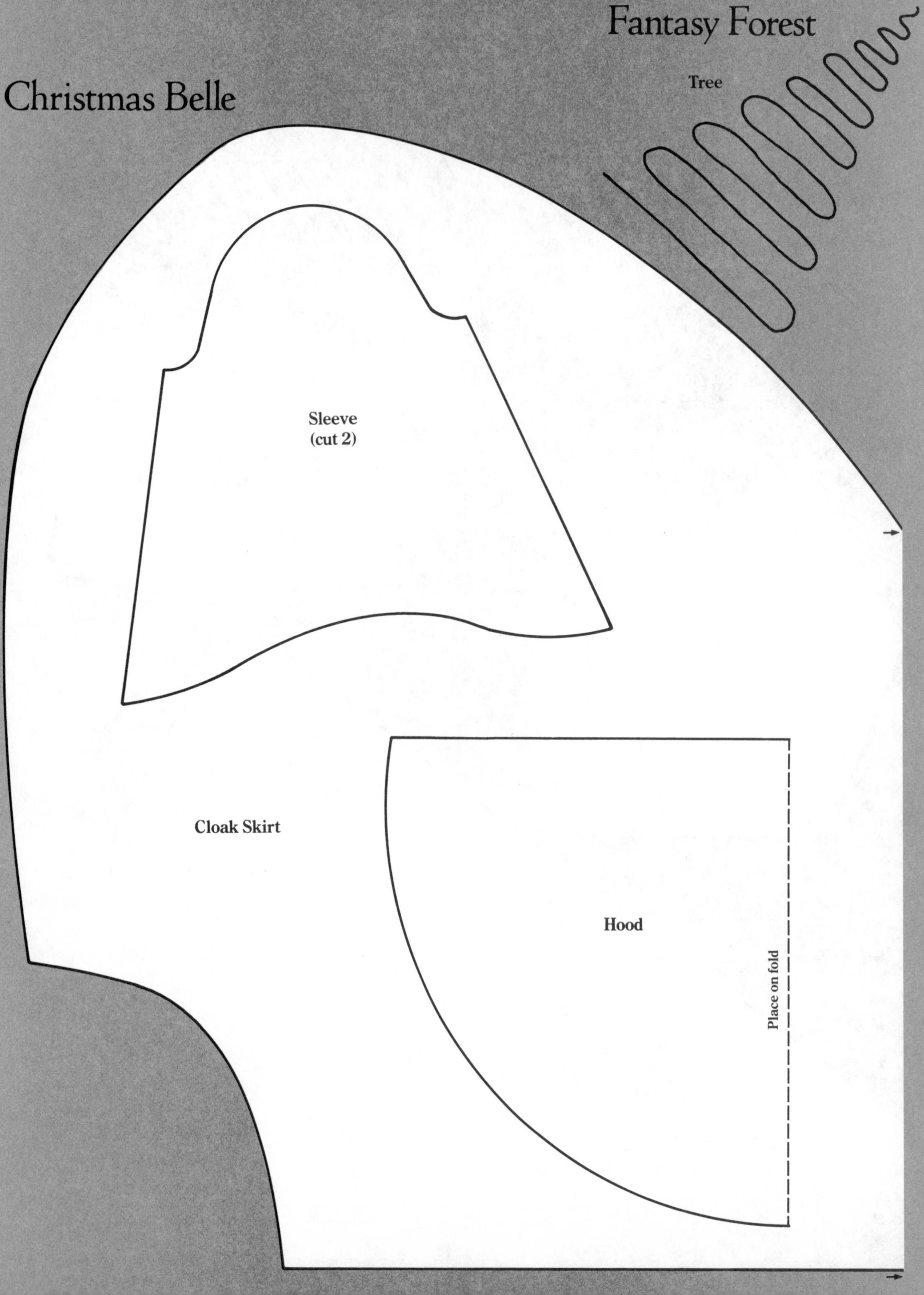

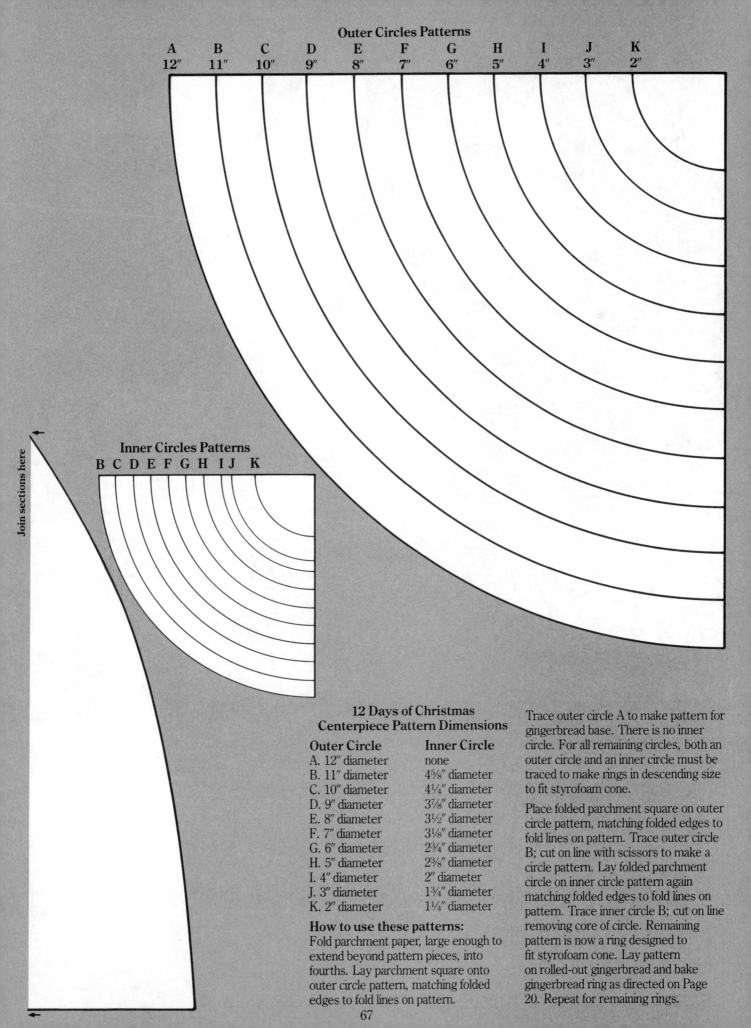

Outer Circles Patterns

A	B	C	D	E	F	G	H	I	J	K
12"	11"	10"	9"	8"	7"	6"	5"	4"	3"	2"

Join sections here

Inner Circles Patterns

B C D E F G H I J K

**12 Days of Christmas
Centerpiece Pattern Dimensions**

Outer Circle	Inner Circle
A. 12″ diameter	none
B. 11″ diameter	4⅝″ diameter
C. 10″ diameter	4¼″ diameter
D. 9″ diameter	3⅞″ diameter
E. 8″ diameter	3½″ diameter
F. 7″ diameter	3⅛″ diameter
G. 6″ diameter	2¾″ diameter
H. 5″ diameter	2⅜″ diameter
I. 4″ diameter	2″ diameter
J. 3″ diameter	1¾″ diameter
K. 2″ diameter	1¼″ diameter

How to use these patterns:
Fold parchment paper, large enough to extend beyond pattern pieces, into fourths. Lay parchment square onto outer circle pattern, matching folded edges to fold lines on pattern.

Trace outer circle A to make pattern for gingerbread base. There is no inner circle. For all remaining circles, both an outer circle and an inner circle must be traced to make rings in descending size to fit styrofoam cone.

Place folded parchment square on outer circle pattern, matching folded edges to fold lines on pattern. Trace outer circle B; cut on line with scissors to make a circle pattern. Lay folded parchment circle on inner circle pattern again matching folded edges to fold lines on pattern. Trace inner circle B; cut on line removing core of circle. Remaining pattern is now a ring designed to fit styrofoam cone. Lay pattern on rolled-out gingerbread and bake gingerbread ring as directed on Page 20. Repeat for remaining rings.

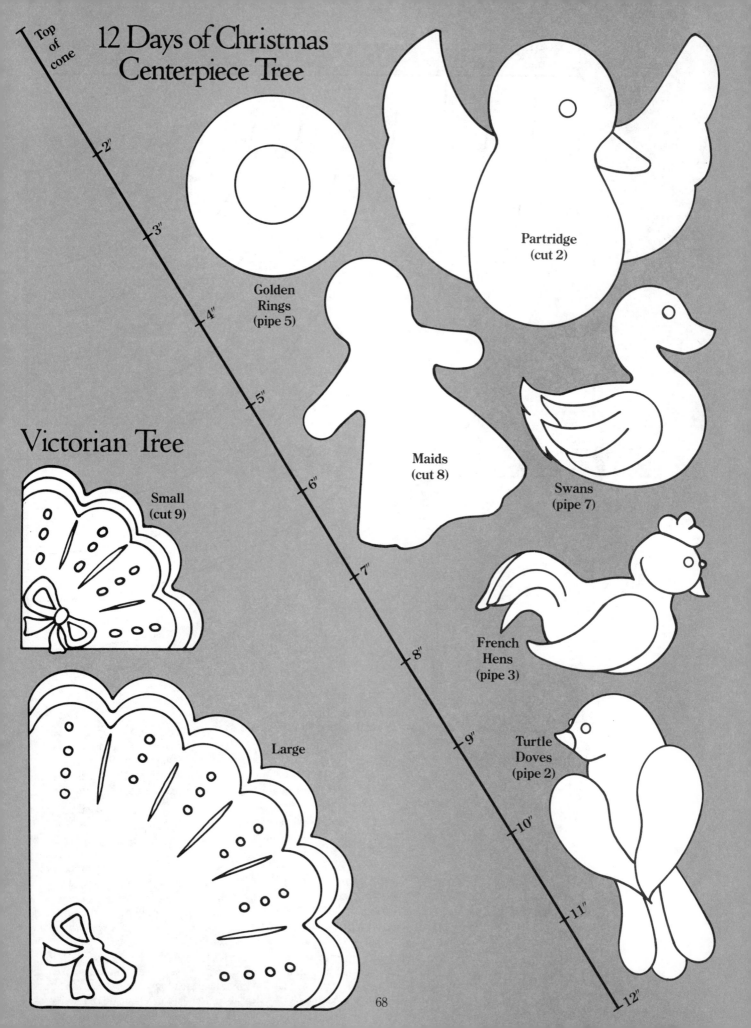

12 Days of Christmas
Centerpiece Tree

Top of cone

2"
3"
4"
5"
6"
7"
8"
9"
10"
11"
12"

Golden
Rings
(pipe 5)

Partridge
(cut 2)

Maids
(cut 8)

Swans
(pipe 7)

French
Hens
(pipe 3)

Turtle
Doves
(pipe 2)

Victorian Tree

Small
(cut 9)

Large

Holly Bear

Gift

Cookie Luminarias

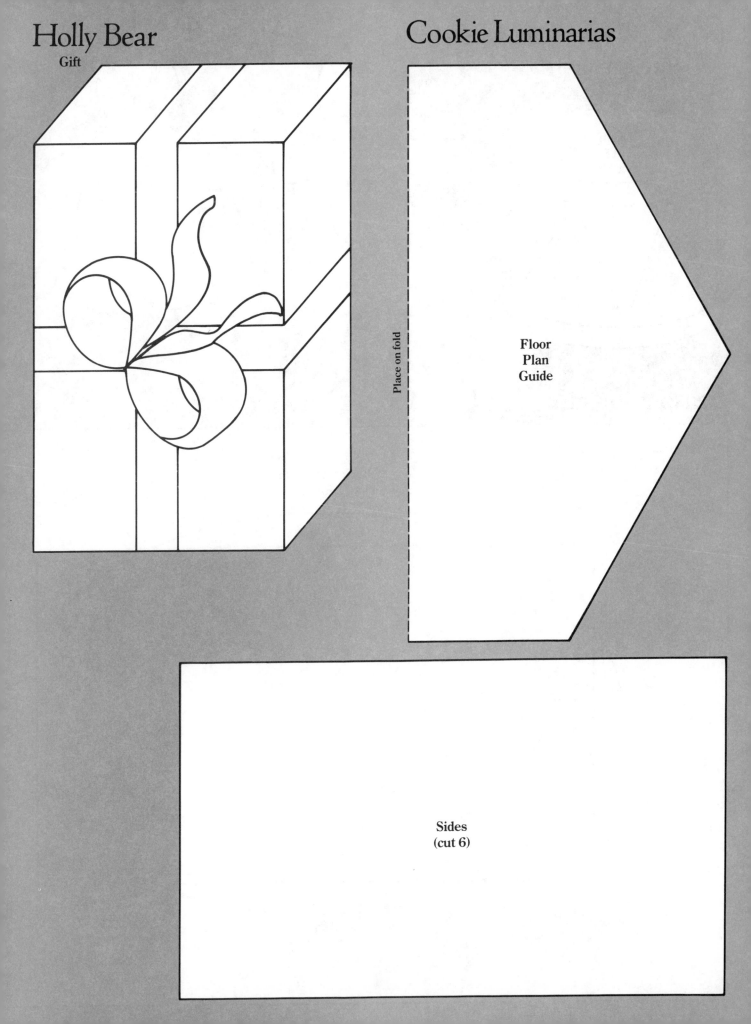

Place on fold

**Floor
Plan
Guide**

**Sides
(cut 6)**

12 Days of Christmas Centerpiece Tree

Drum
(cut 9)

Ladies
(cut 11)

Lords
(cut 12)

Season's Greeting Cards

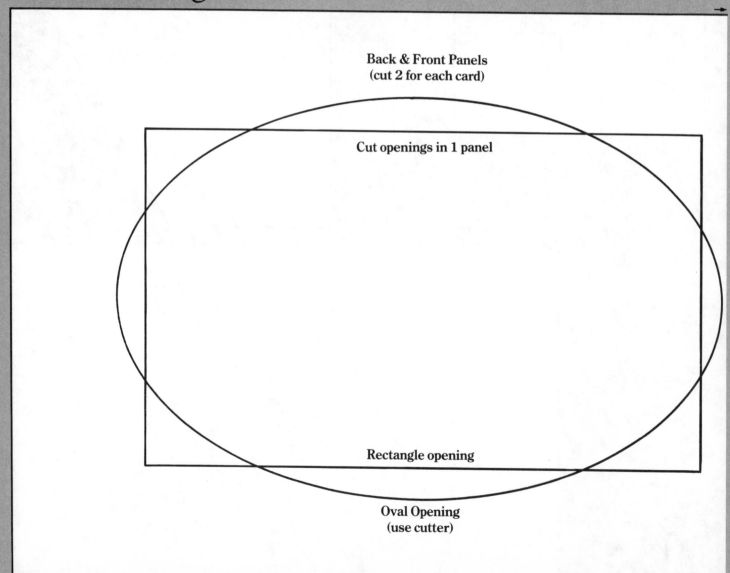

Back & Front Panels
(cut 2 for each card)

Cut openings in 1 panel

Rectangle opening

Oval Opening
(use cutter)

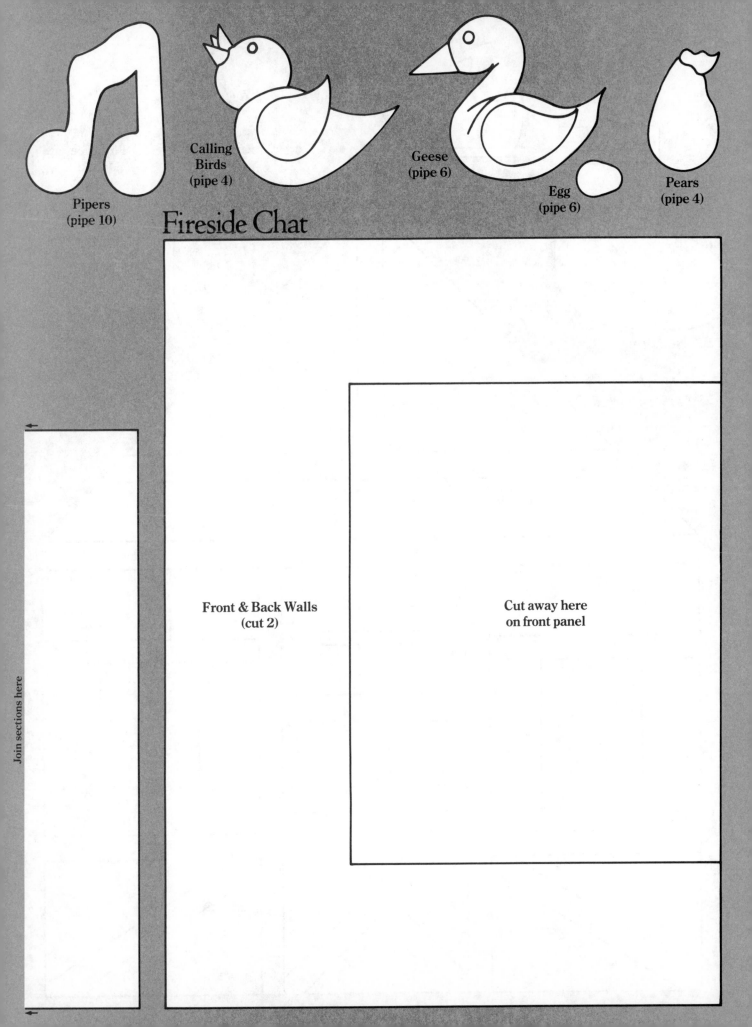

Pipers
(pipe 10)

Calling
Birds
(pipe 4)

Geese
(pipe 6)

Egg
(pipe 6)

Pears
(pipe 4)

Fireside Chat

Join sections here

Front & Back Walls
(cut 2)

Cut away here
on front panel

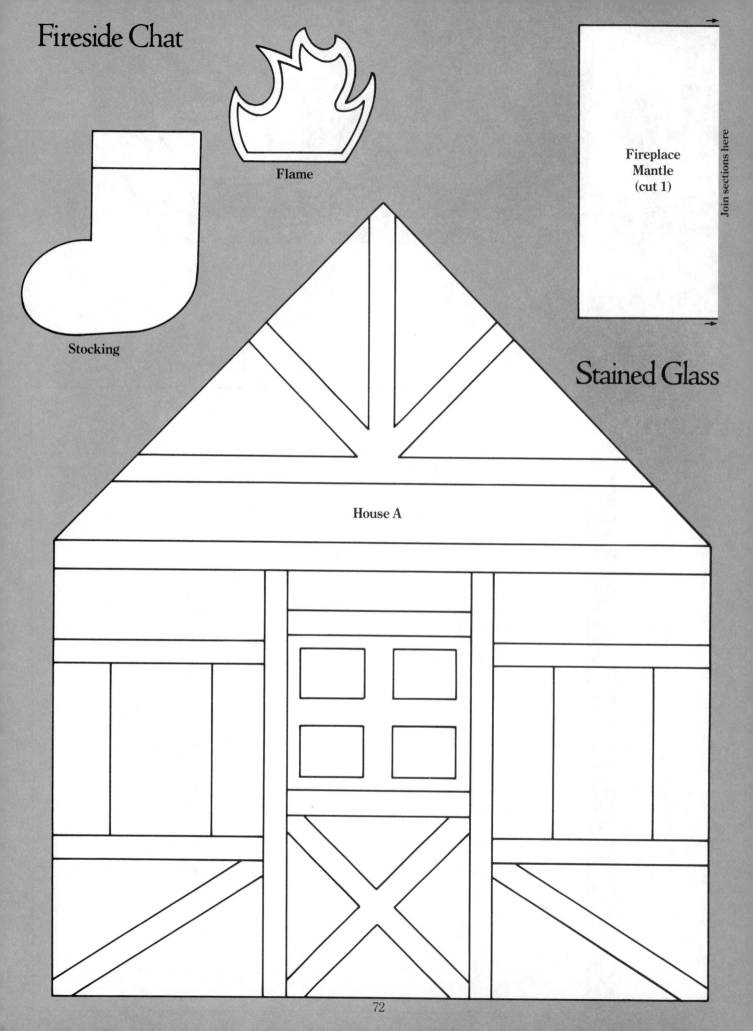

Fireside Chat

Flame

Fireplace
Mantle
(cut 1)

Join sections here

Stocking

Stained Glass

House A

Fireplace Side Walls
(cut 2)

Tudor Village

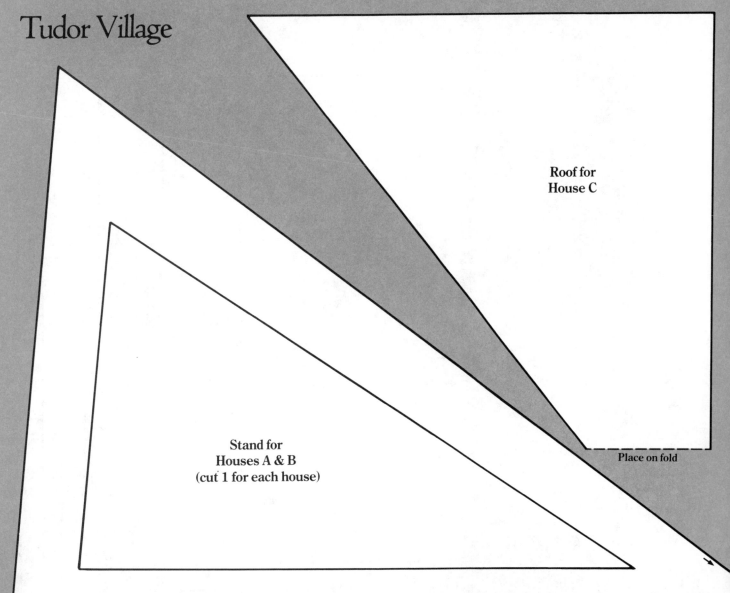

**Roof for
House C**

**Stand for
Houses A & B
(cut 1 for each house)**

Place on fold

**Stand for House C
(cut 1)**

**Draw lines
to a point**

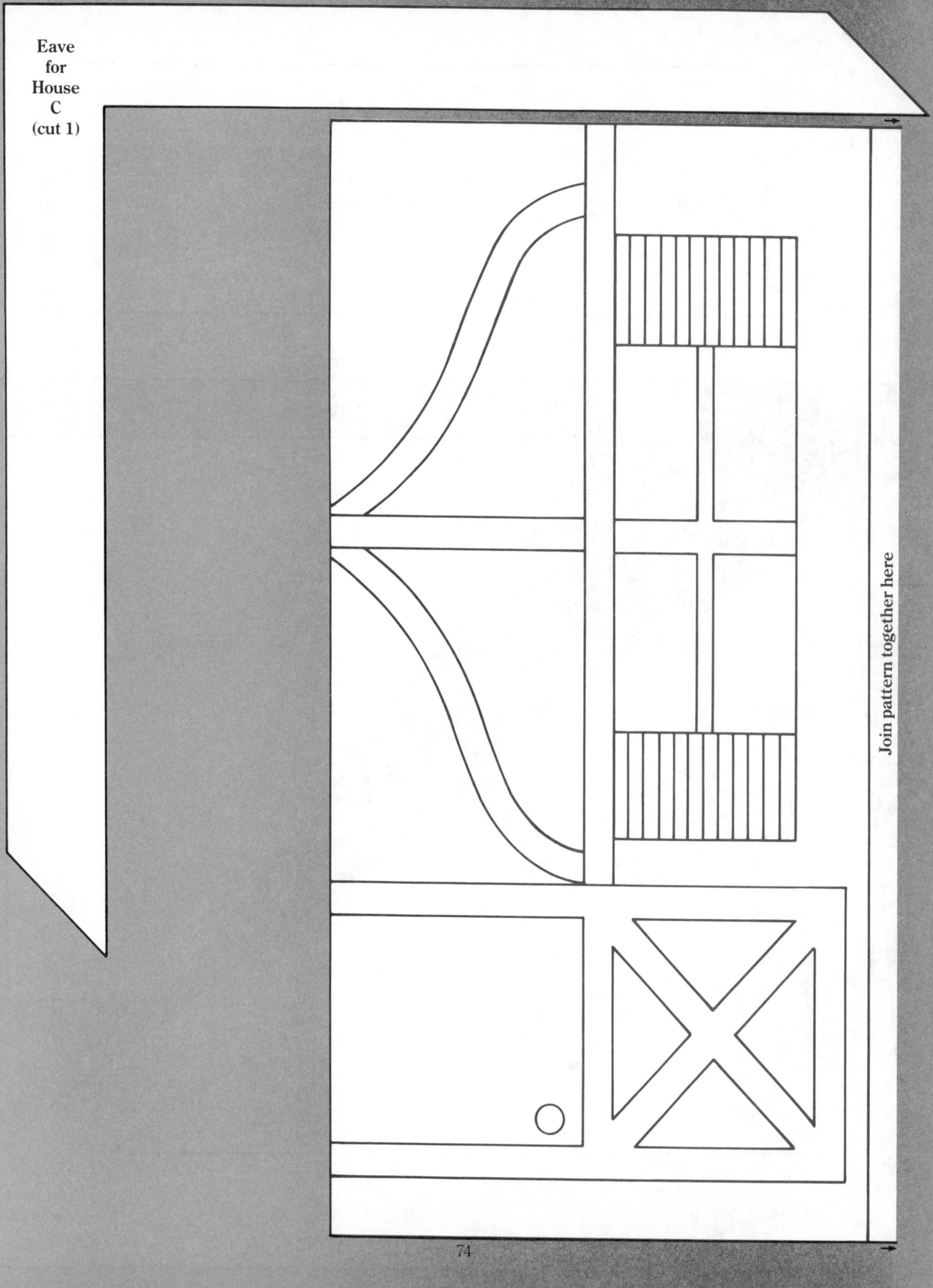

Eave
for
House
C
(cut 1)

Join pattern together here

74

Stained Glass Tudor Village

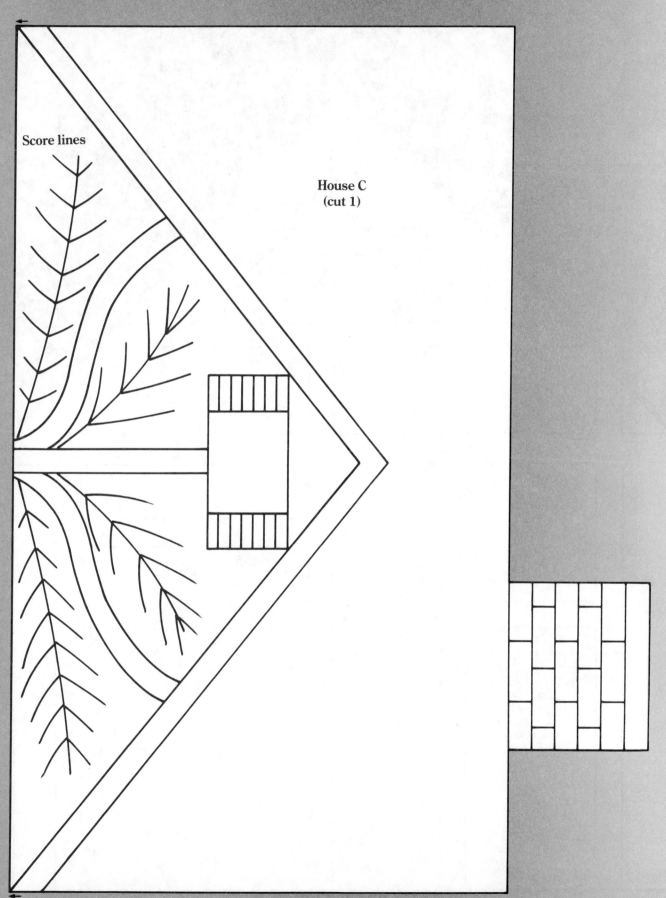

Score lines

House C
(cut 1)

Window

House
B
(cut 1)